1,001 BEST PLACES TO HAVE

SEX IN AMERICA

JENNIFER HUNT AND DAN BARITCHI
Founders of *AskDanAndJennifer.com*

A WHEN, WHERE, AND HOW GUIDE

Avon, Massachusetts

Published by
Adams Media, a division of F+W Media, Inc.
57 Littlefield Street, Avon, MA 02322. U.S.A.
www.adamsmedia.com

ISBN 10: 1-60550-053-4
ISBN 13: 978-1-60550-053-9

Printed in the United States of America.

J I H G F E D C B A

Library of Congress Cataloging-in-Publication Data
is available from the publisher.

This publication is designed to provide accurate and authoritative information with
regard to the subject matter covered. It is sold with the understanding that the publisher is
not engaged in rendering legal, accounting, or other professional advice. If legal advice or
other expert assistance is required, the services of a competent professional person should
be sought.

—From a *Declaration of Principles* jointly adopted by a Committee of the
American Bar Association and a Committee of Publishers and Associations

Many of the designations used by manufacturers and sellers to distinguish their prod-
uct are claimed as trademarks. Where those designations appear in this book and Adams
Media was aware of a trademark claim, the designations have been printed with initial
capital letters.

Certain sections of this book deal with activities that may be potentially hazardous, dangerous, or illegal. The authors, Adams Media, and F+W Media, Inc. do not accept liability
for any injury, loss, legal consequence, or incidental or consequential damage incurred by
reliance on the information or advice provided in this book.

This guide is for entertainment purposes only.

This book is available at quantity discounts for bulk purchases.
For information, please call 1-800-289-0963.

Contents

Acknowledgments

So many people helped make this book a reality, and we would like to extend our profound and sincere gratitude to each of them.

Paul Carlson, who has inspired and served as our personal mentor and guide over the years (*www.PersonalChanges.com*); Lennel Fajardo, who takes care of all the details so that we don't have to; Kaylen Shubrick, our incredible senior editor and writer; Mike Hendricks and Melody Brooke, who kindly provided the Sex Quiz for this book and some great additions to the list of places to have sex (*www.ThisIsGreatSex.com*); The Beautiful Kind, who kindly provided the excellent Kink Quiz for this book (*www.TheBeautiful Kind.com*). And of course, Neil Salkind (*www.studiob.com/salkindagency*), our amazing literary agent; and our publisher Adams Media (*www.adams media.com*), for their help and support while writing this book.

And last, but not least, we extend our profound thanks to you for reading this book. We hope you have as much fun reading it as we did writing it!

Introduction

Most couples enjoy incredible sex in the beginning of a relationship, but it doesn't take long for them to fall into that same boring, predictable slump that we all know so well. You have sex less and less often, and it eventually becomes more of a chore than an exciting, uplifting adventure.

So why does this happen? It's simple really. People usually limit their love-making to a few well-known places and positions. Not surprisingly, before too long, the novelty and excitement wears off, you get a little bit lazy, and fall into a rut. And then, seemingly without reason, you wake up one day wondering why you never have sex anymore.

But it doesn't *have to* be that way! It is possible to have an incredible sex life, even long after the initial infatuation has worn off. Each day *can* truly be an opportunity to explore new, uncharted, exotic sexual adventures with your partner. You just have to decide you want it.

Once you've made that decision, you need a plan, some ideas to actually make it happen—ideas that are fun, fresh, exciting, and most of all, different from your worn out, everyday routine. That's where our book can help you.

1,001 Best Places to Have Sex in America explores the most popular and exciting places where you can explore your sensuality, break through sexual barriers, and truly spice up and revive your sex life—starting right now!

Each "place" is rated in terms of sexual satisfaction, physical effort involved, kink level, and risk. These ratings will help you determine which sexual locations best fit into your lifestyle and personal comfort zone.

ECSTASY FACTOR:
Measure of how erotic and sexy the place is.

CALORIE BURN:
How physically demanding each position or place is.

KINK LEVEL:
How far this place or position will push a person's
boundaries of what society considers being "normal" sex

RISK:
Your chances of getting injured, "caught," or otherwise
embarrassed, humiliated, or arrested.

We've also provided the pros and cons of each "place" so that you know what you're getting in to. And as an added bonus, there's even a recommended sexual position to try. For detailed descriptions of each of the positions and how to execute them, look in Appendix A—Our Top Twenty-Five Sex Positions.

We suggest you pick your top 100 places and commit to try each of them over the coming year. You'll be surprised at the incredible results!

Dan and Jennifer
AskDanAndJennifer.com

CHAPTER 1

100 PLACES TO HAVE SEX AROUND THE HOUSE

Sex should not be limited to your bedroom. The following is a list of 100 places around your house to have sex with your partner. Make it a goal to try each and every one of them.

1. On the Roof under the Stars

Are you looking for a nice private location to get away from it all? Grab a bottle of wine, a blanket, and a few pillows and make your very own observatory on the roof.

BEST POSITION Missionary or Deck Chair

PROS The view and the privacy.

CONS If you have a really steep roofline, this could be quite dangerous—especially if you drink too much. So be careful.

2. On the Deck (or Patio) under the Stars

Not brave enough or crazy enough to climb up on the roof? Then simply head out to the deck or patio to enjoy a romantic evening under the stars.

BEST POSITION Missionary or Deck Chair

PROS It's a romantic way to enjoy each other outside and yet it's still somewhat discreet (unless you live in a city and you're on a shared deck).

CONS Your view may be obstructed by trees or rooflines.

3. On the Deck (or Patio) in Full Sunlight

Sun is a natural aphrodisiac, so get naked on your deck or patio and enjoy yourselves in the afternoon sun.

BEST POSITION Missionary or Deck Chair

PROS Ten to fifteen minutes of sunlight per day is actually good for you—just avoid the midday hours when the UV rays are their strongest.

CONS You'll have to get over your shyness around being naked in broad daylight (if you have any!).

4. In the Pool Shed

There's just something incredibly erotic about a quickie in the pool shed.

BEST POSITION Bodyguard or Dancer

PROS It's private and easily accessible.

CONS It can be messy and disorganized, so stick with standing positions. Also be careful of any sharp tools or uncompleted projects that might be lying around.

5. While Swimming in the Pool

If you have a swimming pool in your backyard, and you never have sex there, stop reading and join us again when you're finished. If you're not lucky enough to have a pool in your backyard, don't miss the opportunity next time you're spending the night with someone who does.

BEST POSITION Dancer or Delight

PROS There's just something about swimming naked that gets us all excited.

CONS Sex in the water can require more coordination than you think.

6. On the Sun Tanning Ledge in the Pool

Fooling around on the tanning ledge is a great way to stay cool without getting fully submersed in the water.

BEST POSITION Mastery or Cowgirl

PROS You can stay cool while you work up a sweat with each other.

CONS The water reflects the sun's rays creating faster sunburn, so if you're playing during the day, don't forget the sunscreen.

7. On the Diving Board

If you're lucky enough to have a pool with a diving board instead of a "play pool" (no deep end), then the diving board is a great place for some steamy outdoor sex.

BEST POSITION Cowgirl or Mastery

PROS Typical diving boards are just high enough off of the ground to give you a great angle for penetration.

CONS Diving boards can be very hard and rough—so make sure you put down a beach towel or blanket.

8. On a Floating Raft in the Pool

This is another variation on the tanning deck, but you'll need to make sure that your raft can support the weight of two.

BEST POSITION Missionary or Cowgirl

PROS You can have fun bouncing around on the raft.

CONS It won't be very stable so be careful not to fall off.

9. In the Hot Tub in the Backyard

If you have a hot tub in your backyard, then what are you waiting for? Hot tubs are even more fun if there's more than two.

BEST POSITION Delight or Spread Eagle

PROS Everyone wants to get naked in the hot tub!

CONS Water is simply not a lubricant and it will break down most water-based lubricants.

10. Under the Waterfall of the Pool in Your Backyard

Whether you have a waterfall in your home pool or you're thinking about having one built, an incredibly romantic way to break it in is to have sex underneath it.

BEST POSITION Dancer or Delight

PROS Duh! A waterfall in your own backyard!

CONS You could get water in your eyes and nose.

11. In Your Backyard Fountain

A backyard fountain can be a great place for a little bit of afternoon nookie. Don't have a fountain? Then shoo the birds out of the bird bath and bend over.

BEST POSITION Delight or Standing Doggy Style

PROS It's very spontaneous.

CONS Small fountains can be a little challenging.

12. In a Lounge Chair in the Backyard

This is one of my favorite places to have sex around the house. There are so many things you can do with a simple lounge chair. And it's very freeing to being naked on the patio.

BEST POSITION Drill or Riding the Face

PROS Comfortable and spontaneous.

CONS Cheap lounge chairs can be downright dangerous!

13. On Your Patio Table Underneath a Giant Umbrella

String lights around your giant umbrella and plan romantic dinner. After the dishes have been cleared (or in the middle of cleaning the dishes), sprawl yourselves on the table for a spontaneous romp.

BEST POSITION Standing Doggy Style or Butterfly

PROS There's just something incredibly erotic about being spread on the table like a buffet.

CONS You may break the table, but if you do, that just means the sex was really worth it!

14. In a Hammock in the Backyard

If you have a hammock in your backyard, it can be the perfect place for an afternoon sex session. Just be sure to avoid tipping yourself out!

BEST POSITION Missionary or Drill

PROS Having sex in a hammock can make you feel like you're on vacation on a beach somewhere!

CONS It's easy to fall out of a hammock—just a little motion can send you and your partner to the ground.

15. On a Slip N' Slide in the Backyard

You may be thinking . . . a Slip N' Slide—really? But it can actually be quite fun. The trick is to actually use the Slip N' Slide as foreplay. And then after you're all wet and grassy leave the Slip N' Slide on while you have a romp in the water.

BEST POSITION Missionary or Cowgirl

PROS It's a totally unique way to experience sex in the outdoors.

CONS Rocks can be painful, so make sure that you clear the path before getting started.

16. In the Kiddie Pool in the Backyard

Take a break from the yard work and splash around with one another in the kiddie pool—grownup style.

BEST POSITION Doggy Style or Deck Chair

PROS It's a great to take a break and cool off.

CONS Be careful not to damage the pool or you'll have some explaining to do when the little ones get home from school.

17. While Standing on the Ladder to the Attic

If you have ladder access to your attic, it can be a great place to fool around. It puts one of you up higher than the other which is great for oral sex and manual stimulation.

BEST POSITION Standing Oral or Manual Stimulation

PROS It puts your partner at the perfect height.

CONS The ladder may not support the weight of both of you so be careful.

18. In the Attic in the Heat of Summer

If you're the type of person who likes to get really sweaty during lovemaking, then venture up to the attic for a quickie in the heat of the summer.

BEST POSITION Dancer or Bodyguard

PROS It's like a built-in sauna.

CONS There's a real danger of heat exhaustion, so don't stay up there too long.

19. In the Attic During a Thunderstorm

If you've ever been in the attic during a thunderstorm, you know it's a great way to feel closer to nature without actually going outside.

BEST POSITION Dancer or Bodyguard

PROS It's a great way to experience the storm without being out in the elements, especially if you have windows in your attic that let the lightning shine through.

CONS Not all attics have flooring put in. If this is the case make sure to take a big blanket or try standing position to avoid getting the insulation on your skin.

20. On the Patio During a Thunderstorm

If you're looking for a closer connection to nature, venture out on the patio during a thunderstorm for an electric lovemaking session.

BEST POSITION Missionary or Deck Chair

PROS The smell of the rain and sound of the storm invigorate your senses.

CONS Make sure your patio is covered or you are low to the ground to reduce the risk of getting struck by lightning.

21. In the Storm Shelter

Looking for a private hideaway? Then look no further than the storm shelter in your backyard. Who knows, you may find this to be your favorite private retreat. Don't forget the candles!

BEST POSITION Anything goes—depending on the size of your storm shelter!

PROS It's dark. It's cozy. It's private. What more could you want?

CONS Spiders, bugs, and dirt!

22. On the Swing Set in a Swing

There are several positions that you can try in the swing itself. You can sit in it, straddle it, and bend over it just to name a few.

BEST POSITION Delight or Mastery

PROS There are so many possibilities for positions and creativity.

CONS It is outside so the neighbors may see—but this could actually be a positive if you're an exhibitionist.

23. On the Slide of the Swing Set

The slide can be another interesting sex toy. You can lie on it and bend over the ladder. Use your imagination.

BEST POSITION Standing Doggy Style or Missionary

PROS It's right there in the backyard.

CONS Make sure the slide is sturdy enough to support both of you—it was designed for kids' play, not adult play.

24. In a Tent in the Backyard

Remember when you were a kid and you would love to set up the tent and have a sleepover in the backyard? Well, it's even more fun as a grownup.

BEST POSITION Missionary or Cowgirl

PROS It's a getaway that you can take any time you like.

CONS You will be outside so bring the mosquito spray.

25. On the Trampoline in the Backyard

Lying on a trampoline under a full moon with a blanket and some pillows—you have the makings of a romantic rendezvous.

BEST POSITION Cowgirl or Mastery

PROS You can use the slight bounce of the trampoline to make these positions even more fun.

CONS Once again you're outside, so bring the mosquito spray.

26. Under the Trampoline in the Backyard

To get a whole new perspective of your backyard similar to what your kids and pets see, lie down under the trampoline for a roll in the grass.

BEST POSITION Missionary or Doggy Style

PROS It's like being in a make-believe fort.

CONS There's low headroom so you'll have to stick to positions that are low to the ground.

27. In a Treehouse in the Backyard

If you have a treehouse, it can be a great location for an afternoon tryst. Just make sure that you're back in the house before the kids get home from school.

BEST POSITION Deck Chair or Cradle

PROS It's private and cozy.

CONS Treehouses can be quite small. And make sure it can hold the weight of two adults!

28. In the Gazebo in the Backyard

There are few things more romantic than a gazebo, a full moon, a bottle of wine, and a few candles. When your gazebo is in your backyard it's even better.

BEST POSITION Mastery or Lap Dance

PROS This is an incredibly romantic place to spend some private time with your partner.

CONS You're outside and most gazebos are not very private.

29. While Barbequing in the Backyard Wearing Nothing but an Apron

Enjoy an adult BBQ for two by cooking dinner and fooling around outside wearing nothing but aprons. It'll be so fun running around with your bottoms exposed!

BEST POSITION Standing Doggy Style and Lap Dance

PROS You'll either work up a good appetite or forget dinner all together.

CONS Don't' lean against the grill—it's hot!

30. Behind the Bushes in the Backyard

Get a little kinky in your backyard by having a quickie in the bushes.

BEST POSITION Doggy Style or Dancer

PROS It's creative and sneaky.

CONS Hopefully your bushes are well pruned because they can be very poky.

31. Behind the Bushes in the Front of the House

Take it up a notch by having sex behind the bushes in the front of your house.

BEST POSITION Doggy Style or Dancer

PROS If the neighbors stop by, you can just tell them you were inspecting the hedges.

CONS The front of the house can be much more visible and you may have uninvited spectators.

32. On the Grass under the Sprinklers in the Backyard

There's just something about having sex in the rain. But there's no need to wait for the next rainstorm. Simply turn on the sprinklers and make your own rain shower, day or night.

BEST POSITION Missionary or Dancer

PROS Getting wet in all kinds of ways.

CONS It can be cold after a while, especially at night.

33. On the Grass under the Sprinklers in the Front Yard

Depending on your front yard and how adventurous you feel, you can "play in the rain" in the front yard.

BEST POSITION Missionary or Cowgirl

PROS Your neighbors will be so jealous! They just wish they had your sex life.

CONS This may count as indecent exposure. Check with a legal counsel.

34. In the Kids' Playhouse in the Backyard

The kids' playhouse is a great place to sneak away for a quickie. If you're having a dinner party, no one will ever look for you there. Just be careful not to bump your head.

BEST POSITION Deck Chair or Lotus

PROS It's out of the way.

CONS Depending on the ages of your children, playhouses can be quite small.

35. In Your Kids' Sandbox

Remember your honeymoon on the beach? Bring back those memories in your own backyard. Take a beach towel and pull the lid off that plastic turtle. Mommy and daddy need some play time!

BEST POSITION Doggy Style or Cradle

PROS It's fun to play in the sand and pretend you're at the beach.

CONS The plastic turtle sandboxes are not very big.

36. Under Your Pergola

String your pergola with lights and step outside on a romantic summer evening for a night to remember.

BEST POSITION Missionary or Dancer

PROS This can be incredibly romantic.

CONS You're outside, so bring the bug spray.

37. Up Against the House in the Side Yard

This is a great place for a quickie and a break from the yard work. Being dirty and sweaty makes this one even more fun—maybe you can reward your husband or wife by surprising him or her after yard work or some gardening.

BEST POSITION Dancer or Standing Doggy Style

PROS Very spontaneous and primal.

CONS If you don't like being dirty and sweaty this one may not be for you.

38. On the Basement Floor

It might not be very adventurous, but having sex in your basement can provide a nice change of scenery every once in awhile if you don't want to go too far from home.

BEST POSITION Standing Oral or Delight

PROS You don't even have to leave home.

CONS Traditional basements are often chilly and have their share of spiders, crickets, and mildew.

39. On the Basement Stairs

Tackle your partner on the way up the stairs for an incredible quickie.

BEST POSITION Game's On or Delight

PROS It's very spontaneous.

CONS Basement stairs are not always carpeted so be careful not to injure yourself or your partner.

40. On the Bathroom Counter

Sit her on the bathroom counter for quick tryst before work. If your counter's not big enough just bend her over.

BEST POSITION Delight or Standing Doggy Style

PROS It's easy and very raunchy.

CONS You may be late for work.

41. On the Bathroom Floor

Lie down on the bath mats and enjoy!

BEST POSITION Missionary or Doggy Style

PROS You can jump back in the shower when you're finished.

CONS Watch out for rug burn.

42. On the Bathroom Toilet

The toilet is a great place for girl-on-top sex. Make sure to put the lid down.

BEST POSITION Lap Dance or Mastery

PROS Toilets are normally just the right height so that both of your feet will touch the floor.

CONS Some people may consider this a little icky.

43. In the Bathtub

This is a great opportunity to take a bubble bath together.

BEST POSITION Cradle or Mastery

PROS It's as good as a hot tub and you can play with the bubbles and splash water and still have great sex.

CONS If your bathtub is small it can be challenging to find a comfortable position.

44. In the Shower

Having sex in the shower is like having sex under a waterfall, only better—especially if you're lucky enough to have a shower with a built in bench. This opens it up for many more positions.

BEST POSITION Dancer or Standing Oral

PROS You can control where the water flows by moving the showerhead.

CONS If you get too excited you may slip and fall, so be careful!

45. On the Bed in the Bedroom

OK, this is a no-brainer, the bed is the number one place that people have sex. Your bed is soft, comfortable, and warm. It's the first place that most people think of to have sex, but why not try something other than Missionary position in the dark? Turn the lights on. Throw the covers on the floor or replace them with leather or satin.

BEST POSITION Try them all and then learn some more.

PROS The privacy of your home and the sky's the limit.

CONS Beware of getting complacent and doing the same thing all the time. This is a sure recipe for boredom.

46. On the Bedroom Floor

The floor is hard and cold even if you have carpet, yet it's incredibly erotic. If you need some padding, go ahead and pull the pillow and comforters on the floor, just don't get in bed!

BEST POSITION Doggy Style and 69

PROS Pretty much anything you can do in the bed, you can do on the floor.

CONS The floor and be quite hard and rug burn is a definite possibility.

47. Under the Bed

This is a great opportunity for some role play. You can pretend that you're having an affair and your spouse came home early. You and your secret lover must hide under the bed until they leave.

BEST POSITION Spoons or Missionary on your side

PROS Role play can be great fun!

CONS Your bed literally may not have enough ground clearance.

48. On the Dresser in the Bedroom

Don't forget about your dresser. You can lie on it or over it or just lean up against it.

BEST POSITION Doggy Style and 69

PROS Your dresser can be used as a replacement for a table in the bedroom. It's a great way to provide additional support or to raise your partner to a new height.

CONS Don't break the mirror. That could mean seven years of bad luck! (If you believe in that kind of stuff . . .)

49. In the Bedroom on a Huge Stack of Pillows

This one brings back the memories of those huge piles of leaves when you were a kid. Find every pillow in the house and throw them on the bedroom floor—and dive in!

BEST POSITION Riding the Face and Spread Eagle

PROS Putting lots of pillows on the floor is softer and also allows you to use pillows to support various positions.

CONS You may get feathers in your mouth.

50. In the Master Bedroom Closet in the Dark

For some reason this just brings out the bad boy and bad girl in all of us. Master bedroom closets are usually very dark, which can serve to free us from our daylight inhibitions.

BEST POSITION Standing Oral and Bodyguard

PROS It's very dark.

CONS It's very dark—don't bump into anything.

51. In the Bedroom on a Liberator Wedge

If you've never tried a Liberator Wedge, go out and buy one or two or three. They come in all shapes and sizes and allow you to try many sex positions that you may not otherwise be flexible or strong enough to try.

BEST POSITION Now you can try them all.

PROS Did you read the description?

CONS Liberator Wedges can be expensive.

52. On the Top Bunk of Your Kid's Bunk Bed

Remember the nostalgia of the top bunk when you were a kid? Bring it back in a very fun, very adult way!

BEST POSITION Missionary and Drill

PROS Even though it's just the top of a bunk bed, being elevated above everything else gives you a little rush.

CONS Be careful not to fall off!

53. On the Dining Room Table

There's a reason that all of these steamy movies show people having sex on a large table or desk, it's just incredibly erotic!

BEST POSITION Standing Doggy Style or Butterfly

PROS Dining room tables can be very sturdy. Especially the solid wood variety.

CONS Wooden dining room tables can be hard, and be careful of fragile glass-top tables.

54. In the Dining Room on a Chair

While the dining room table puts the woman in a compromising position, the dining room chair can do the same—in a good way—for the man. Just think of all of the things you can do to him while he's tied to the dining room chair.

BEST POSITION Cowgirl or Game's On

PROS The chair provides support for a lot of different angles and positions.

CONS Just don't fall out of the chair.

55. Under the Dining Room Table

Having sex under dining room table will provide you with an entirely new perspective of your dining room.

BEST POSITION Missionary or Spread Eagle

PROS It's a lot like a private clubhouse.

CONS Watch out for rug burn.

56. In the Exercise Room on an Exercise Ball

Exercise balls are not only great for strength and flexibility; they can serve as a replacement for a Liberator Wedge if you don't have one.

BEST POSITION Cradle or Doggy Style

PROS You can try all kinds of new positions and angles.

CONS They are round so they roll—don't roll off.

57. In the Exercise Room on the Exercise Bench

The exercise bench is almost as good as the lounge chair. Even though it's a little smaller and not quite as comfortable, it still provides great support for all types of positions.

BEST POSITION Cowgirl or Riding the Face

PROS The exercise bench is in your own house so there are no privacy concerns like there would be at a public gym.

CONS Exercise benches can be very narrow.

58. In the Exercise Room Standing Against the Weight Machine

This one's fun for a little bondage play. Have her stand up and put her wrists through the curl loops, connect them to the lat pull and have your way with her (make sure to add enough weight to support her)

BEST POSITION Dancer or Bodyguard

PROS If you have an in-home gym, you have your own built in dungeon!

CONS Just be careful of the weights and tables. The machine wasn't really built to be a dungeon.

59. In the Family Room in a Rocking Chair or Glider

Use the momentum of the rocking chair to take some of the stress off your muscles. You'll be able to last even longer this way!

BEST POSITION Lap Dance or Mastery

PROS If you can get the rhythm, you can go much longer.

CONS You might find squeezing two people into one rocking chair is a little difficult, even if one person is sitting on top of the other!

60. In the Family Room in a Recliner

Recliners are fun in that you can lean them back a little or a lot and some of them even rock. Have fun experimenting with different positions.

BEST POSITION Missionary or Mastery

PROS You can adjust the chair to the angle you enjoy the most.

CONS You husband may not want to mix pleasure with sleeping in the recliner.

61. In the Family Room on the Floor

Once again, anything you can do in the bed, you can do on the floor. This one just feels a little kinkier because you're not hiding behind the bedroom door—you're doing it in the "family room."

BEST POSITION Missionary or Cowgirl

PROS Most family rooms are larger than the bedrooms, so you'll have more room to romp. Just make sure to move the furniture out of the way.

CONS The floor and be quite hard and rug burn is a definite possibility.

62. In the Family Room on the Sofa

The sofa in the family room is a great place for a spontaneous rendezvous. Take a break from watching your nightly sitcom or drama and spend a little time working on what really matters, your relationship.

BEST POSITION Drill or Delight

PROS It's an easy and convenient place to have sex. No planning required.

CONS If you have little ones they could walk in, but at least they'll grow up knowing their parents love each other and like to "wrestle."

63. In the Family Room Behind the Sofa

Remember what we did under the bed? Pull the sofa out just enough for you both to fit behind it. It should be very tight—that's the whole idea.

BEST POSITION Spoons or Missionary

PROS It can be fun to role play as you're "hiding" behind the couch!

CONS If your kids find you, this one will be a little challenging to explain. Just tell them you're making a clubhouse.

64. In the Family Room over the Ottoman

Okay, so now let's take the sofa one step further. While the sofa is intimate and cozy, the ottoman is open and adventurous. Sit on it, lie on it, bend over it, you get the idea.

BEST POSITION Doggy Style or Deep Impact

PROS The height of the ottoman and is just right for some great penetration angles.

CONS Like the sofa, you're a little bit exposed for someone who may walk in unexpectedly.

65. In the Family Room in a Teacup Chair

Teacup chairs are all the rage for dorm rooms, but you can put one in your study or den for a great way to get into some unique sexual positions.

BEST POSITION Lotus or Mastery

PROS It's a great way to try some new sitting positions.

CONS You may not be able to get into your favorite positions.

66. On the Entry Stairs

After you've been out on a hot date, the entry stairs are a perfect place for some really steamy, spontaneous sex. Like the bedroom floor, it has the feeling of "We just couldn't wait."

BEST POSITION Deck Chair or Doggy Style

PROS Very spontaneous.

CONS It may not be comfortable because most of the surfaces in the foyer are hard and angular.

67. In the Foyer Against the Front Door

Turn on the exhibitionist in you by having sex with your partner right smack in the middle of your foyer. If you really want spice it up, leave the front door open and have sex in the open doorway.

BEST POSITION Dancer or Standing Oral

PROS It's incredibly erotic and passionate.

CONS The neighbors might see you, but is that really a con?

68. In the Foyer on the Floor

You may find yourself sliding down the wall and onto the floor. That's perfectly okay so long as you're enjoying yourselves.

BEST POSITION Missionary or Cowgirl

PROS It's still incredibly erotic and passionate.

CONS Hopefully the pizza delivery man doesn't show up at the wrong moment!

69. In the Coat Closet

If you're worried about the neighbors, step into the coat closet. Now you have a reason to finally clean all the stuff out of there.

BEST POSITION Dancer or Bodyguard

PROS Unique and cozy.

CONS It can be a very tight squeeze.

70. In the Crawl Space under the Stairs

Think of it as your own private club. Remember what it was like when you were a kid to create a clubhouse under the stairs? You can even have your own secret password and initiation ritual.

BEST POSITION Missionary or Cowgirl

PROS The kids will never look for you there!

CONS Hope the kids did not create their clubhouse first.

71. On the Front Porch Swing

Oh, the romance of sitting together on the front porch swing. Enough romance already! It's time to get down and dirty on the swing. Use the motion of the swinging to add some momentum to your swing!

BEST POSITION Lap Dance or Standing Doggy Style

PROS If you can get the rhythm, this can really be a lot of fun.

CONS If you don't get the rhythm, you could end up with a black eye or busted nose.

72. Against the Front Door or Porch Column

Yet another chance for some role play. You can pretend that your boyfriend has just brought you home and your parents are waiting just inside—so you'll have to be really quiet so that you don't get grounded for the rest of your life!

BEST POSITION Dancer or Bodyguard

PROS Spontaneity.

CONS The neighbors may not approve.

73. In the Game Room on a Beanbag Chair

Beanbag chairs also make a great substitute for a Liberator Wedge. You can try all sorts of new positions that you may not otherwise be able to get into because of flexibility or strength.

BEST POSITION Deep Stick or Leg Glider

PROS Lots of new positions.

CONS Be careful not to pop the beanbag or you'll be cleaning up lots of little beads.

74. In the Game Room on the Pool Table

There's just something about drinking beer and lying out across the pool table that says, "I'm a slut." So embrace your inner slut and have fun. You know you want to! Don't be embarrassed. It's OK to let go a little or a lot—especially in the privacy of your own home.

BEST POSITION Standing Doggy Style or Butterfly

PROS It's a great opportunity to let go of some of your inhibitions.

CONS You can really mess up the felt on your pool table with lubricant and other various liquids.

75. In the Game Room on a Bar Stool

This is a great extension of the pool table. Why not make a night of it enjoy every piece of furniture in your game room?

BEST POSITION Delight or Standing Doggy Style

PROS A bar stool provides good support for many of the standing positions.

CONS Be careful not to fall off a stool.

76. In the Kitchen on a Bar Stool

A bar stool can make a great prop for sex in the kitchen, too. You can sit on it, lean on it, lie over it, and even stand on it. The possibilities are endless.

BEST POSITION Delight or Standing Doggy Style

PROS A bar stool provides good support for many of the standing positions.

CONS Be careful not to fall off a stool or otherwise injure yourself, especially if the stove is on or there are knives lying around.

77. In the Garage on the Hood of Your Car

Hey, this always works in the movies right? Having sex on the hood of you car can be extremely arousing and exciting. Just make sure that you do it before you drive across town and the engine heats up.

BEST POSITION Butterfly or Deep Impact

PROS The feel of cold hard steel is nice on your skin.

CONS Burns from a hot engine are a possibility.

78. In the Garage, in the Car

When you get home from a hot date, there's no need to wait until you get in the house to make mad passionate love. Stay in the car! But remember to turn it off.

BEST POSITION Cowgirl or Mastery

PROS Everyone loves the feeling of "I can't wait, I want you now!"

CONS It's not as comfortable as a bed but can be just as passionate.

79. In the Garage in a Refrigerator Box or Shipping Crate

Hey, we all have our kinks! Make sure to use the "box," not the refrigerator. You can actually get locked into a refrigerator or freezer and suffocate—don't do that.

BEST POSITION Dancer or Bodyguard

PROS It does have that clubhouse feel to it.

CONS It may be challenging to find a box that's big enough.

80. In the Garage on the Workbench

Ladies, are you tired of your man working in the garage all the time? You know what they say, "If you can't beat 'em, join 'em!"

BEST POSITION Delight or Game's On

PROS Instead of getting mad at your man, you can get happy.

CONS Oil and grease can stain your clothes.

81. In the Guest Room on an Air Mattress

The feeling of sleeping on top of air is blissful enough, now how about making love? You'll feel like you're having sex on a cloud. Also, being in the guest room is similar to being at a hotel so it can feel like a mini-vacation.

BEST POSITION Missionary or 69

PROS It's like a bed, but it's not the "same ol'" bed.

CONS Be careful not to pop the air mattress.

82. In the Guest Room on the Pull-Out Couch

Your guests probably have sex on your pull out couch, why can't you? You and your partner can have a good chuckle every time a guest stays over—just remember to change the sheets.

BEST POSITION Cowgirl or Deck Chair

PROS Similar to the air mattress, only more durable.

CONS Pull-out couches are traditionally uncomfortable. Save the sleep for your own bed—this is about sex.

83. In Your Home Office on the Desk

If you're tired of working, let your partner slide your papers off your desk and put you on it instead! It's also a great opportunity for some role play. Haven't you always wanted to be the boss and naughty secretary?

BEST POSITION Butterfly or Standing Doggy Style

PROS It's a great break from the workday.

CONS You may not want to get back to work. Is that really a con?

84. In Your Home Office Against the Filing Cabinet

If you've already tried the desk, opt for some standing positions against the filing cabinet, wall, or whiteboard. Standing positions have a way of feeling even more spontaneous and naughty.

BEST POSITION Dancer or Bodyguard

PROS You don't have to mess up the desk.

CONS If you have a short two- or three-drawer filing cabinet, be careful not to knock it over or fall off.

85. In Your Home Office under the Desk

This one is really great if you have one of those big wooden desks. Crawl under and give your partner some oral action while he or she is working.

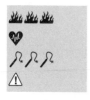

BEST POSITION Game's On or Manual Stimulation

PROS A very high excitement factor because it just feels like you're getting away with something.

CONS You may lose a client if you're not careful.

86. In Your Home Theater Room on the Sofa

Not everyone has a home theater, but if you do, it can be the perfect place to make out—and more! To ramp up the excitement even more, turn on a porno and do whatever comes naturally.

BEST POSITION 69 or Drill

PROS It's like being at the movies, but with more privacy.

CONS If you do this one too much it can get boring, so think of new positions and movies to keep it exciting.

87. In Your Home Theater Room in Front of the Projector

Take your movie experience to the next level. Turn on a good porno (or just the projector lights) and enjoy watching yourselves have shadow sex.

BEST POSITION Standing Doggy Style or Standing Oral

PROS Very sexy and voyeuristic.

CONS It can be challenging to make the shadows look just right, especially if you're trying to "follow" a porno.

88. In Your Home Theater Room on the Floor While Watching Raunchy Porn

The floor is just more primal than the sofa. Besides you have more room to wrestle around!

BEST POSITION Cowgirl or Doggy Style

PROS You can get rowdy and roll around on the floor.

CONS The floor can be hard and rug burn is always a concern.

89. In Your Giant Soft Armchair in Front of the Fire

It's cliché but romantic—cuddling with your partner on a hugely soft armchair in front of a warm fire is something you definitely don't want to miss.

BEST POSITION Game's On or Lap Dance

PROS It's a beautiful and romantic way to spend the night alone with each other after the kids have gone to bed.

CONS Don't scoot the armchair too close to the fire!

90. In the Kitchen over the Breakfast Table

Take a break from the same old boring breakfast routine and have each other for breakfast.

BEST POSITION Butterfly or Standing Doggy Style

PROS It's a great way to work up an appetite.

CONS Some people may have an issue with bodily fluids on the breakfast table.

91. On the Kitchen Counter

We've already talked about bending over a barstool while cooking, but why not include each other as the appetizer. Try sitting on the cabinet and experimenting with some food play.

BEST POSITION Standing Doggy Style or Game's On

PROS This is an easy way to mix food and sex, if you like that kind of thing.

CONS Watch out for any knives that may be lying around on the counter.

92. In the Kitchen Pantry

Move aside the cans of green beans and boxes of cereal for a new way to do the quickie in the kitchen.

BEST POSITION Dancer or Bodyguard

PROS New scents and aromas can really invigorate the senses.

CONS Depending on how large your pantry is, you may or may not have enough space.

93. In the Kitchen over the Breakfast Bar

Two words—"Breakfast Buffet." Lay your partner out on the breakfast bar and decorate him or her with whatever you're going to have for breakfast.

BEST POSITION Missionary or Spread Eagle

PROS What a way to wake up! It's better than a cup of coffee!

CONS The breakfast bar can feel cold to skin, so put a towel or blanket down to make it more comfortable.

94. In the Kitchen on the Cold Tile Floor

Nothing says "Take me" like sex on the cold hard floor.

BEST POSITION Missionary or Spread Eagle

PROS Yes it's hard and uncomfortable, but in this case, that's what makes it so appealing.

CONS This is an evening activity—it's too harsh to do first thing in the morning.

95. In the Laundry Room on or over the Ironing Board

Make doing the laundry fun and exciting instead of a boring chore by throwing your partner over the ironing board for a quickie.

BEST POSITION Standing Doggy Style or Standing Oral

PROS As you can see, it sparks a lot of creativity.

CONS Your ironing board may not hold much weight. Be careful!

96. In the Laundry Room on Top of the Washing Machine While It's Running

This is just one of those positions that everyone should try once. It's more of a cliché that anything else, but if you catch the spin cycle just right, you never know . . .

BEST POSITION Standing Doggy Style or Spread Eagle

PROS It definitely makes laundry day more exciting.

CONS Washing machines these days are too tall to really sit on and do anything other than oral.

97. In the Living Room on Top of the Coffee Table

You can really have fun with this one! Try everything from a quickie when you're home alone to creating an appetizer buffet for one or many.

BEST POSITION Butterfly or Deep Impact

PROS Coffee tables are normally at a great height for Deep Impact.

CONS Too much weight might crack or break the table. If he's on his knees, make sure to put a pillow or soft blanket under his knees to prevent rug burn.

98. In the Living Room with the Curtains Wide Open

Release your inhibitions and say good morning to the neighbors in a whole new way!

BEST POSITION Standing Doggy Style or Bodyguard

PROS You're still in the safety of your home, besides, they shouldn't be peeking in your windows anyway.

CONS The nosy neighbor across the street may suddenly become speechless. Wait, that's not really so bad, is it?

99. In Your Loft Overlooking the Lower Level of Your Home

Your loft can be a super romantic and sexy place to make love to your partner while looking down on the rest of your home.

BEST POSITION Standing Doggy Style or Bodyguard

PROS It can be a private way to let go of your inhibitions.

CONS If you're leaning up against the rail, you definitely run the risk of falling off.

100. In the Mudroom

Mudrooms are where things are dirty, so why wouldn't you want to get dirty with your partner there? Next time it's raining outside, forget the umbrella, and have a quickie as soon as you come inside while you're both still dripping wet.

BEST POSITION Dancer or Bodyguard

PROS It's very spontaneous.

CONS The floor may be slippery, so be careful not to fall.

CHAPTER 2

BEST ROMANTIC PLACES

We all like romance in some form or other, so we included the following places to satisfy the romantic in all of us.

101. At a Ski Lodge by a Huge Fireplace

While everyone else is out on the slopes, you and your partner can stay in and hang out by the fire with some wine or hot cocoa. Enjoy your bodies silhouetted by the fire.

BEST POSITION Missionary or Lotus

PROS It's warm, cozy, and incredibly sexy.

CONS You may miss the best powder of the trip.

102. In a Beach Grotto

Take a trip to Fern Grotto Beach, Santa Cruz, California. The ferns of this incredible beach grotto hang down, wrapping you in secluded privacy for you and your partner to enjoy a romantic and sensual encounter.

BEST POSITION Missionary or Dancer

PROS It's a beautifully romantic way to spend a spring or summer afternoon.

CONS There are things in the water that bite and sting.

103. At a Secluded Cabin in the Woods

It's a bit cliché, but incredibly romantic! Nestle up with a cup of hot chocolate in a woodsy cabin and let your romantic side take over. This is a great opportunity to really "make love."

BEST POSITION Missionary or Spoons

PROS Take a moment to enjoy the absolute privacy.

CONS No TV or computer to distract you. But try not to think of it as a con, you have each other!

104. On the Deck of a Yacht in the Middle of the Ocean During a Full Moon

Charter a yacht (or at least a large sailboat) for the weekend and spend an evening making love on deck under the moonlight.

BEST POSITION Deck Chair or Deep Stick

PROS The moon and stars appear much brighter when you get away from the city lights.

CONS Chartering a boat can be expensive. Consider going in with some friends.

105. Deck of a Cruise Ship at Night

Take an Alaskan cruise and enjoy the view of your partner's silhouette against the coastline.

BEST POSITION Standing Doggy Style or Bodyguard

PROS The view is incredible.

CONS You're well north of the equator, and it's cold on deck!

106. On the Fourth of July Underneath a Huge Fireworks Display

What a romantic way to celebrate our country's Independence Day! Make love to your partner underneath the booming, colorful fireworks for a night to remember.

BEST POSITION Missionary or Spoons

PROS It's a very romantic way to see the fireworks.

CONS The really great fireworks displays can be crowded. Opt for sitting in a large field rather that in the middle of the crowd.

107. In a Gazebo at the Park in the Moonlight

You're getting that sitting under the full moon is romantic, right? Take a stroll through the park and take a break at a gazebo when the moon is high. You can even bring a picnic basket and some wine.

BEST POSITION Mastery or Missionary

PROS It's a romantic interlude away from the house.

CONS You're in a public park so check your surroundings.

108. On a Gondola Ride up a Mountain

Whether you're skiing, dining, or just sightseeing, take a gondola ride up the mountain for a romantic get away. We're not talking about a ski lift, but an enclosed gondola.

BEST POSITION Mastery or Missionary

PROS You can enjoy the beautiful scenery both inside and outside of the car.

CONS It may be a little challenging to get a multipassenger car to yourselves—this is where your tipping skills come in handy.

109. In a Horse-Drawn Carriage on a Cold Winter Night

Take a ride through the city in a horse-drawn carriage. Snuggle up under the blanket for a romantic and potentially very erotic ride around town.

BEST POSITION Mastery or Game's On

PROS No one, except maybe the driver, will know what you're doing so relax and have fun. Just make sure to leave a big tip!

CONS You may end up with a chatty driver. Politely tell him that you'd like some privacy.

110. In a Penthouse with a Panoramic View of the City

The view alone is awe inspiring. Make it even better by adding some romance of your own. Bring candles, champagne, massage oil, and your best lingerie to make this a night to remember.

BEST POSITION Anything goes!

PROS It's like a one-night honeymoon.

CONS Penthouse rooms can be expensive, but look around in the off-season for some great deals or cash in your airline miles for an upgrade.

111. At the Four Seasons in Beverly Hills

While the pool area is a bit lacking, the spa and the service they provide make this one of the most romantic places to spend the night or a weekend.

BEST POSITION Try them all.

PROS The service is incredible and the house car is a Mercedes 500 (they'll be happy to take you wherever you want to go).

CONS Sorry guys, but the pool is lame—time for a remodel!

112. At the Four Seasons in Dallas, TX

This is our favorite local retreat! Stay in the bungalows along the Byron Nelson golf course. It's private and the view is beautiful.

BEST POSITION Try them all.

PROS The service and friendly staff cannot be beat.

CONS Unless you're a huge golf fan, avoid going during the Byron Nelson Golf Tournament—it's too crowded.

113. At the Four Seasons in Maui, HI

It's a gorgeous hotel on a beautiful island and if the service is even close to the other Four Seasons, then you may never come back!

BEST POSITION Try them all.

PROS Duh—it's in Hawaii.

CONS It's in Hawaii, so for most of us, it's more of a major vacation than a weekend getaway.

114. In a Romantic Victorian House

Gorgeous paintings and fabulous architectural designs set the mood off right when you're looking for a night of romance. Look for a romantic bed and breakfast in your area.

BEST POSITION Anything goes!

PROS It's less expensive than a penthouse.

CONS You may not be the only couple staying at the bed and breakfast, so you'll have to keep it down to avoid disturbing the neighbors.

115. Candlelit Room

There's nothing more romantic than a room literally filled with candles. Not three candles on the dresser—go out and buy 50 or 100 candles. An easy way to do this is with tea light candles. They typically come in packages of 100. And then add in a few pillar candles for variety.

BEST POSITION Anything goes!

PROS This is an incredibly romantic and erotic way to spend the evening.

CONS One hundred candles can be a fire hazard. Take the appropriate precautions, like not putting lit candles on the bed or carpet, keeping them away from drapes and bedding, and not leaving them unattended while lit.

116. On the Shore of a Beautiful Secluded Lake

In America, it doesn't get more beautiful than Lake Tahoe. With more than seventy-two miles of shoreline, surely you can find the perfect spot.

BEST POSITION Missionary or Lotus

PROS You have incredible views of the lake.

CONS It can get very cold in the evenings so bring a sleeping bag and dress in layers.

117. On a Balcony with a Dozen Wind Chimes

You may find this incredibly romantic or just annoying. If you're in the first group, then fill your balcony or porch with wind chimes and spread out on a comfy sleeping bag for a truly romantic evening.

BEST POSITION Missionary or Cowgirl

PROS You can do this at home.

CONS If it's too windy, it can be downright loud so avoid the really loud wind chimes and stick with the softer sounds.

118. On a Dark Amusement Park Ride Such as "The Tunnel of Love"

While a bit cheesy, a tunnel of love ride can remind you that being together is just as important as your hectic schedule. Take the time for yourselves.

BEST POSITION Mastery or Lap Dance

PROS It's really dark so no one will see what you're doing.

CONS The ride doesn't last very long, so you'll have to act fast or ride through several times with escalating intensity.

119. On a Hayride in the Fall

A hayride at night with a little bit of sexy action is a wonderful way to celebrate the fall!

BEST POSITION Game's On or Manual Stimulation

PROS It's cold outside so you are expected to cuddle.

CONS It's similar to a horse-drawn carriage ride only more bumpy and public.

120. During a Romantic Christmas Sleigh Ride

Bring the joy of the season to your partner's sweet spots and tease them sensually while riding on a romantic sleigh ride.

BEST POSITION Game's On or Lap Dance

PROS It's a beautifully romantic and sensual way to spend the holiday.

CONS It's cold out so dress warmly.

121. In Big Soft Bed Covered with Rose Petals and Satin Sheets

This one is really for the ladies and it will win her heart every time. When she comes home from work to find you in nothing but a towel holding her favorite glass of wine with a trail of rose petals leading to the bedroom, she'll surely grin from ear to ear.

BEST POSITION Missionary or Spread Eagle

PROS She'll remember your thoughtfulness for years to come—in a good way.

CONS Preparation time and potential for injury from swallowing rose petals.

122. In the Suite of a Luxurious Five-Star Hotel

Spend the night or a weekend in a luxurious hotel. No one caters to your needs like the Four Seasons or the Ritz. Once you've really been catered to, you'll never want to stay anywhere else.

BEST POSITION Anything goes!

PROS Being waited on hand and foot is wonderful.

CONS Prepare to shell out several hundred dollars per night.

123. On a Kissing Bridge

In the old days, Kissing Bridges were covered bridges that were the perfect place to stop and steal a kiss or a hug from your partner. Bring back the tradition in a more modern and liberal way!

BEST POSITION Dancer or Bodyguard

PROS It's romantic and a great stop to break up a monotonous road trip.

CONS They're quite old—make sure the one you pick is sturdy enough to hold you and your partner's weight.

124. Next to an Old, Rustic Watermill

Get a little nostalgic and go back to the colonial era by planning a day trip to an old water mill. Oh, and while you're there, what a great opportunity to get some great sensual photos!

BEST POSITION Dancer or Standing Doggy Style

PROS It's sweet, romantic, and sexy all at the same time!

CONS The water mill may be on private property so watch for signs.

125. On a Screened-in Porch During a Thunderstorm

If you have a screened-in porch, this is a great opportunity for some impromptu, primal sex, and lots of romantic cuddling afterward as you both listen to and feel the storm subside around you.

BEST POSITION Mastery or Missionary

PROS The wonder of getting romantic with your partner and feeling connected with nature at the same time.

CONS Comfort could be an issue if your patio furniture is not padded. The neighbors could get a peek—it's only a con if you mind that sort of thing.

126. Under a Rainbow

The rainbow symbolized the end of the storm, a symbol of peace and hope. Take a few minutes after a storm passes to remember what you're thankful for—including your partner and the incredible sex that you enjoy!

BEST POSITION Missionary or Lotus

PROS Take the chance to renew your love for one another.

CONS You can't really get *under* a rainbow.

127. Under a Natural Waterfall

There's something so magical, romantic, and sexual about having sex underneath or behind a waterfall. Let the water pour over your naked bodies like nature intended!

BEST POSITION Dancer or Standing Doggy Style

PROS Having sex under a waterfall is extremely exhilarating.

CONS The reason it's exhilarating is because the water is freezing!

128. Underneath an Ornate Crystal Chandelier

Let the light from a sparkling crystal chandelier show off your best assets while you make love to your partner underneath. It's romantic, sensual, and a little bit naughty, all rolled into one.

BEST POSITION Missionary or Deck Chair

PROS The light from a chandelier is diffused, soft, and flattering.

CONS You may have to move the furniture that is normally highlighted by the chandelier.

129. Underneath Your Flower-Covered Trellis

There's a reason so many people get married underneath a trellis dripping with flowers—it's incredibly romantic!

BEST POSITION Dancer or Standing Doggy Style

PROS Being underneath a flower-covered trellis can transport you to your very own Garden of Eden!

CONS If you get too frisky, you might knock down the trellis.

130. Underneath Your Lit Christmas Tree

There's something so sensual and romantic about having sex underneath a lit Christmas tree, and giving your partner pleasure is the best holiday gift you can give.

BEST POSITION Missionary or Spoons

PROS What a way to celebrate the beauty and harmony of the holiday season!

CONS Be careful not to shake the tree, or you might have ornaments falling on your heads.

131. At a Movie in the Park

Rather than going to the same old movie theater, take a romantic detour and see a movie in the park. You can cuddle together under a blanket and watch a good movie and play footsies under the covers.

BEST POSITION Missionary or Spoons

PROS It's a romantic way to spend an evening at the park.

CONS Depending on the setup of the event, you may or may not be able to lie down together.

CHAPTER 3

BEST PLACES
FOR A QUICKIE

It seems like we're all so rushed for time these days! While it's important to make the time to nurture your relationship both emotionally and sexually, a quickie every day is better than not having sex with your partner because you're waiting for the perfect romantic evening.

132. On the Exam Table at Your Doctor's Office

What better fantasy than to play the naughty doctor or nurse and the patient. What a racy way to have a quickie before the doctor comes in! Given the time that it takes most doctors to get to the exam room, it may not even need to be a quickie.

BEST POSITION Deck Chair or Standing Doggy Style

PROS It will help you to release inhibitions by having sex in a semi-public place.

CONS You might get caught, and you might leave behind evidence that the doctor finds in his own exam.

133. On the Exam Table at the Gynecologist's Office

Continuing with the doctor theme, the gynecologist's table provides even better access for some great oral sex or deep insertion positions.

BEST POSITION Deep Impact or Spread Eagle—feet in the stirrups

PROS This is a great opportunity to try some new positions, heights, and angles on the adjustable bed.

CONS Let face it. Upon examination, the doctor will know exactly what you've been up to.

134. In the Waiting Room at the Doctor's Office

If you're the first patient of the morning, get there early and enjoy a quickie while you're waiting for them to unlock the office.

BEST POSITION Standing Doggy Style or Bodyguard

PROS It makes a boring wait more enjoyable.

CONS They may not actually have the waiting room unlocked so you may have to stand in the hall.

135. On the Roof at the Hospital

Take the stairs up to the roof and see what you can find. You may be surprised to find picnic table and chairs to play on.

BEST POSITION Standing Doggy Style or Bodyguard

PROS It's a great excuse to check out the rooftop. Think about it—how often do you visit the roof of the buildings you go into? Maybe you should.

CONS The roof access may be locked. Or you might not be the first to think of going up there.

136. In the Stairwell of the Hospital

Can't make it to the roof? Have fun in the stairwell.

BEST POSITION Standing Doggy Style or Bodyguard

PROS Stairwells are just excellent places to grab a quickie.

CONS Pick a less busy stairwell so that you're not disturbed.

137. On a Hospital Elevator

They're *so* slow that you may actually have some time to get it on. Assuming, of course, that you don't stop on any of the other floors. . . .

BEST POSITION Dancer or Bodyguard

PROS It's a very slow-moving elevator and if you use a staff elevator, you may not have to make any additional stops.

CONS You are in a hospital, so watch out for germs.

138. In an Empty Hospital Room

Go to the hospital and look for an empty room on a quiet floor—not the emergency room. Close the curtains and have fun.

BEST POSITION Missionary or Cowgirl

PROS If someone comes in, you can just say that you were looking for a place to take a quick nap.

CONS There may not be any sheets on the bed, but look around in cabinets and closets, you'll probably be able to find some.

139. In a Hospital Supply Closet

Being in the hospital doesn't have to be all doom and gloom, especially if you're only visiting. Sneak off into a supply closet and have a quickie with your partner.

BEST POSITION Dancer or Standing Doggy Style

PROS Some hospitals supply closets come fully equipped with pillows and blankets.

CONS Most hospital supply closets are locked so it may be a little tricky to find an open one. And let's not forget Biohazard Waste—watch out for needles.

140. In the Aquarium Section of the Pet Shop

Your visit to your local pet shop doesn't have to be as boring as just picking up pet food!

BEST POSITION Standing Oral or Dancer

PROS The aquarium section of a pet shop is usually a very secluded place and you'll get the feeling you're in the ocean with the fish when you're actually just blocks from home sweet home.

CONS Be careful not to tip over or break any aquariums!

141. On the Roof of Your High School During a Reunion

The high school gym is open for the reunion, and so are most doors inside the building. Climb through the roof access stairs and have your way with your lover. Bring your wine and a blanket and enjoy!

BEST POSITION Missionary or Deck Chair

PROS Remembering all the guys/girls who thought you were a loser and imagining seeing their faces now.

CONS You may end up as the feature photo in the class reunion photo album.

142. In Your Lawyer's Office

Waiting around for your lawyer to get back from lunch doesn't have to be boring anymore! Have fun on your lawyer's desk, the conference table, or even the couch or chairs in your lawyer's office—if you're made to wait too long, anything is fair game.

BEST POSITION Butterfly or Mastery

PROS An ordinary visit to your lawyer becomes extraordinary with some playfulness with your partner.

CONS Getting caught by your lawyer really kills the mood.

143. In Your Banker's Office

Ever feel taken by the bank? Well now you can at least get some enjoyment from it.

BEST POSITION Butterfly or Mastery

PROS It makes filling out that loan paperwork more bearable.

CONS Hopefully you have an old-fashioned bank— newer banks have open floor plans with glass offices.

144. In Your Accountant's Office

While he's counting your money, you can be counting orgasms.

BEST POSITION Butterfly or Mastery

PROS Let him pay attention to the details while you pay attention to each other.

CONS He may bill you.

145. In Your Therapist's Office

Your therapist does wonders for helping to relieve your stress and tension, but so can your partner.

BEST POSITION Mastery or Doggy Style

PROS Consider it sex therapy.

CONS Your therapist may bill you and ask you how having sex in a public place makes you feel.

146. In Your Neighbor's Pool

While your neighbors are out, hop the fence and have sex in their pool.

BEST POSITION Mastery or Standing Doggy Style

PROS If you don't have a pool, their's is a great substitute.

CONS Check for a motion alarm outside or a pit bull.

147. At Your Neighbor's Housewarming Party

Celebrate the new neighbors with a bang—by banging each other, that is.

BEST POSITION Dancer or Standing Doggy Style

PROS It'll be a fun way to check out their home.

CONS Be careful not to break anything or to get caught. Having sex in their house isn't the most neighborly thing.

148. On Your Neighbor's Patio

After you've had sex in the pool, move to the patio. Make it more fun by taking some flirty pictures and hang them on your wall. When you have the neighbors over for dinner, they'll spend weeks trying to remember when you took those pictures!

BEST POSITION Mastery or Standing Doggy Style

PROS It's hilarious and relatively harmless.

CONS Your neighbors will be very confused if and when they see your photos and you might have some explaining to do.

149. In Your Neighbor's Tool Shed

Thinks it was fun in your own tool shed? Wait until you have a quickie in your neighbor's tool shed. It will take the excitement to a new level.

BEST POSITION Dancer or Standing Oral

PROS It feels so sneaky and juvenile.

CONS Your neighbors may catch you. If that happens you'll either have a good laugh or end up in jail.

150. On a Wood Pile While Your Partner Is Still Sweaty from Chopping Wood

Watching your partner cut wood for the fire while you're inside sipping a cup of hot cocoa is an incredible turn on, so make the most of it! Reward your partner for cutting wood by stripping down, before he even gets the chance to take a shower.

BEST POSITION Standing Doggy Style or Dancer

PROS A hot sweaty man working to chop wood is so barbaric!

CONS Make sure to watch out for splinters and those nasty little ants that like to bore into trees.

151. In Your Parents' Bedroom

Next time you're visiting your parents, sneak into their bedroom for a quickie. They'll never know why you're so giggly at dinner.

BEST POSITION Missionary or Standing Doggy Style

PROS It gives you something to do while at your folks' house for the holidays.

CONS Your parents may walk in. Who will be more embarrassed, you or them?

152. In Your Mother-in-Law's Bedroom

It's one thing to have a quickie in your own parents' room, but what about your in-laws' bedroom?

BEST POSITION Missionary or Standing Doggy Style

PROS This one shows your partner that you'll do anything for him (or her) no matter how embarrassing.

CONS It's one more reason for your mother-in-law to hate you.

153. On Top of a Fire Truck

Next time you see a fire truck parked at a burger place, hop in the back for a quickie while the firefighters are inside having a bite to eat.

BEST POSITION Missionary or 69

PROS It's a great alternative to sex in a normal car!

CONS If they get a call while you're still in the back, you'll have some serious explaining to do.

154. Against the Fire Pole at the Fire Station

It's easier if you work in a fire station, but it's still possible if you don't. Give your man a pole dance on the fire pole! Use the pole for a fun and sexy dance and later to lean up against as you bend over and let your lover in from behind.

BEST POSITION Standing Doggy Style or Dancer

PROS What a naughty way to have quick afternoon or middle of the night sex!

CONS You could be interrupted by a sliding fireman if there's a fire.

155. In an Empty Bunk at the Fire Station While Everyone's on a Call

When the fire station is empty, it's the perfect time to grab a bunk for a quickie. Just like the three bears, the firemen will wonder who's been sleeping in their beds.

BEST POSITION Missionary or Cowgirl

PROS You can start your own four-alarm fire between the sheets!

CONS You may have to deal with that one fireman who stayed behind. Just ask him to join and you'll be fine.

156. On a Fire Escape

Live in an apartment building with a fire escape just outside the windows? Step out there for a quickie while the in-laws are staying for the weekend.

BEST POSITION Bodyguard or Deep Impact

PROS It's a great to get some fresh air and enjoy a sexy rendezvous at the same time.

CONS Make sure that it's a well-maintained fire escape and be careful not to fall off.

157. Straddling a Weight Bench During an Invigorating Workout

Nothing gets your blood pumping like a vigorous workout. Get all pumped up and sweaty in a different way with a quick sex session.

BEST POSITION Cowgirl or Mastery

PROS The weight bench is the perfect height for the cowgirl and other girl-on-top positions.

CONS This could be a little tricky in a public gym.

158. In the Locker Room at the Gym

Hit the showers after a nice sweat at the gym! While you're at it you might as well have a quickie in the locker room. You're better off in the guys' locker room, they might even be into it!

BEST POSITION Cowgirl or Standing Doggy Style

PROS Your endorphins are zooming through your body after a workout, making the sex even better.

CONS It's a public locker room, so not everyone will approve.

159. In the Dentist's Chair

Enjoy your next visit to the dentist. Sounds crazy right? But just think, you can play with different heights and positions in the adjustable chair.

BEST POSITION Cowgirl or Mastery

PROS Most dentist chairs are fully adjustable.

CONS Some dentists have an open office concept so there's very little privacy.

160. In a Back Alley Next Time You're Downtown

Next time you're downtown looking for a parking spot, why not make the best of it and pull into an alley for a quickie in your car.

BEST POSITION Game's On or Manual Stimulation

PROS Perhaps a parking spot will open up by the time you're finished.

CONS Watch out for the bicycle cops. They cruise downtown.

161. On the Bar after Last Call

You're drunk, it's early morning, and it's still dark. Why not get on the bar after last call and have a go?

BEST POSITION Standing Doggy Style or Butterfly

PROS You're inhibitions are already gone, what else do you have to lose?

CONS You could definitely get thrown out of the bar—for life.

162. In the Bathroom at a Liquor Store

Go in for some wine and come out with a smile on your face.

BEST POSITION Dancer or Standing Doggy Style

PROS It's quick and easy.

CONS It's a bathroom, so be careful what you touch.

163. On an Observation Deck

Taking your partner up for a romantic view of the city can instantly turn into a titillating quickie. Overlook the incredible sights of the city and enjoy each other's bodies all at the same time.

BEST POSITION Standing Doggy Style or Bodyguard

PROS If you're the only ones up there, you can really get naked!

CONS It can be dangerous leaning over the railings—keep your feet on the ground!

164. On the Bathroom Floor (Yours or Someone Else's)

Nothing says "I want you" like a raunchy quickie on the bathroom floor after a shower.

BEST POSITION Missionary or Cradle

PROS You can do this one every day.

CONS Don't slip on the wet floor.

165. On the Bedroom Floor (Yours or Someone Else's)

The bedroom floor, yours or someone else's, is a great place for a quickie. Having sex on the floor always implies that you just couldn't wait for the bed.

BEST POSITION Missionary or Doggy Style

PROS Sex on the floor adds an extra layer of excitement.

CONS Watch out for rug burn.

166. In Somebody Else's Winnebago

Next time you're camping, sneak into the neighbors' Winnebago for a quickie.

BEST POSITION Missionary or Mastery

PROS It just feels so naughty!

CONS Make sure that they're out on the lake in their boat so that they don't come back early and surprise you!

167. On the Boat Dock at the Lake

Next time you're out on the boat don't forget to tie off for an adventure on the docks. If your dock of choice has a ladder, it can make for a good time in or out of the water.

BEST POSITION Missionary or 69

PROS There's something so liberating and refreshing about going skinny-dipping at night around a boat dock!

CONS Watch out for splinters and wood-ants—ouch!

168. In the Empty Moving Van Before You Return It on Moving Day

Moving day is exhausting, but save some energy for a little frisky fun in the moving van before you take it back. In the cab of the moving van, in the "mom's attic" in the back or even on the ramp!

BEST POSITION Missionary or Cowgirl

PROS Sex in the moving van is a great way to celebrate the move!

CONS Don't get locked inside the back of the moving van!

169. In a Bank Vault or Safety Deposit Room

What a great opportunity to play cop and robber. Pull the curtain and take turns arresting each other. Given the short amount of time that you have in there, you'll have to take turns next time.

BEST POSITION Dancer or Bodyguard

PROS At least you have a curtain for privacy (and if you're really lucky, a locked room!).

CONS Security cameras are a distinct possibility.

170. In the Garage at a Friend's Party

Parties are just great places to have a quickie. Many people keep the drinks in coolers in the garage. Step out to the garage for a drink and a quickie on the cooler.

BEST POSITION Mastery or Standing Doggy Style

PROS It's very easy to slip out to the garage.

CONS Someone else may get thirsty before you're finished.

171. In the Bathroom at a Friend's Party

Excuse yourself to the bathroom and have your partner meet you there for a quickie. Go to a bathroom with lower traffic, like the one upstairs.

BEST POSITION Mastery or Standing Doggy Style

PROS No one will notice you're missing if you don't stay gone too long.

CONS If it's a busy party, there may be a line for the bathroom. That's OK. They can wait a few minutes.

172. In the Closet at a Friend's Party

It's fun, risky, and totally juvenile. Get back in touch with your inner teen and sneak into the closet for a quickie.

BEST POSITION Dancer or Bodyguard

PROS It's all among friends.

CONS You may find something you regret when playing in someone else's closet.

173. In an Empty Bedroom at a Friend's Party

Take it up a notch and step into an empty bedroom at your friend's party. You'll have more room to move around and, if you're brave enough, try some role play, pretending to be your friends.

BEST POSITION Missionary or Standing Doggy Style

PROS The bedroom is way more comfortable than the closet.

CONS You may stay for more than a quickie.

174. In a Greenhouse

Most greenhouses have more than one greenhouse area, pick one that seems the least used and have a go! It's semi-public but also private, and you get to enjoy being around the lush greenery.

BEST POSITION Dancer or Standing Doggy Style

PROS Get close to nature without leaving the city.

CONS Wobbly greenhouse tables and wet floors.

175. On the Hood of Your Car While on a Date

Before you leave the house, restaurant, or mall, lean on the hood of your car for a quickie. Do it before you leave because if you wait until you arrive at your destination, the hood will be very hot.

BEST POSITION Butterfly or Standing Doggy Style

PROS It's very erotic and sexy. Most men love the idea of a woman sprawled out on the hood of their car.

CONS Be careful not to burn yourself on a hot car or get arrested for indecent exposure.

176. On the Hood of Your Sports Car

Take it to the next level. Seriously, it's one thing to have sex on the hood of a Honda and another thing all together to have sex on the hood of a Maserati.

BEST POSITION Drill or Deck Chair

PROS The hood of a sports car will be lower than the Honda, so sex will be easier.

CONS Sports car engines run very hot, so there's real danger of getting burned.

177. In a Photography Darkroom

You can develop your own sexual fantasy by having sex in a photo darkroom. There's something so mysterious about that red lighting!

BEST POSITION Standing Oral or Dancer

PROS There are plenty of tables and chairs to use, and you can always try Doggy Style or standing up.

CONS If you work in photo development, you could get caught by your boss and fired. It could make it even more interesting though.

178. In a Tanning Bed

The sexy glow you'll get after getting randy in a tanning bed won't be from the bulbs, it will be a natural radiance!

BEST POSITION Missionary or Spoons

PROS At least one side of you will get some rays while doing the deed.

CONS If the tanning bed is on, make sure both of you are wearing UV goggles!

179. In a Spray-Tanning Booth

If you are feeling a little adventurous, go in a spray-tanning booth together. You may have to go through twice to get full coverage. Once facing each other and once facing away from each other.

BEST POSITION Dancer or Bodyguard

PROS It's fun and creative. You'll have great fun explaining why your tan is so uneven.

CONS Don't get the tanning spray in your mouth or other orifices. No telling what's in that stuff!

180. At Your Neighbor's Barbecue

While at your neighbor's barbeque, step around the side of the house or behind some bushes for a quickie. It'll be the best barbeque of the season.

BEST POSITION Mastery or Standing Doggy Style

PROS You'll be really hungry and ready to eat some barbeque when you're done.

CONS If you get busted, everyone else may lose their appetite.

181. At Your Partner's Weekly Poker Game

Spice up your partner's weekly poker game with some oral action under the table. The other guys might suspect what you're doing but they won't actually be able to see anything. If your friends are a little more uptight, maybe you can sneak away to the bathroom for a quickie.

BEST POSITION Game's On or Standing Doggy Style

PROS It'll really rev up your sex life for weeks or even months to come.

CONS This is a one-sided activity that's all about his pleasure, but he'll make it up to you later.

182. Backstage at a Concert

At a rock concert, anything goes, but backstage, *anything* goes. Take advantage of this and really have some fun together.

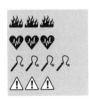

BEST POSITION Lap Dance or Mastery

PROS You can really let loose and have fun.

CONS Watch out for cameras unless you want to end up on next week's episode of *Extra* (blurred out and all).

183. At a Shakespeare Festival

Step back in time a little with your partner by attending a Shakespeare festival. It's like immersing yourself in an entirely different era! You can do it in an alley with your dress hiked up, or Shakespeare-style by making love to your Juliet.

BEST POSITION Mastery or Missionary

PROS Step into a different era and step out of your normal routine.

CONS It's a very public venue with lots of people and children running around, so be aware of your surroundings and respectful of what they may and may not want to see.

184. In a Coat-Check Closet at a Wedding

Weddings inspire romance and a renewed love for our partner as we look back (or ahead) to our wedding day. Step into the coat closet for a romantic quickie.

BEST POSITION Dancer or Bodyguard

PROS In this case, a closet can be romantic.

CONS Hopefully the closet is not filled and overflowing with coats!

185. In an Empty Subway Car

You're sitting there all alone with nothing to do but stare at the empty seats in front of you, so why not make the best of it?

BEST POSITION Mastery or Standing Doggy Style

PROS It's a great way to kill the time on the long subway ride home.

CONS There's always the chance that someone will get on at the next stop, so don't get completely undressed.

186. At Your Local YMCA

The YMCA is a great place to work out. Why not grab a quickie in the locker room after your workout?

BEST POSITION Dancer or Standing Doggy Style

PROS Memberships at the YMCA are typically cheaper than a standard gym membership.

CONS The facilities are typically pretty basic, so finding a corner or private shower may be more challenging.

187. In the Army Barracks

Whether you're in the military or not, having sex in Army barracks can be dirty and quite fun! It's not romantic or sensual, but who doesn't like a nasty quickie every once in a while?

BEST POSITION Standing Oral or Missionary

PROS He'll definitely be standing at attention at the idea of this one.

CONS Getting arrested by the military police is bad for everyone involved.

188. In an Elevator

Having sex in an elevator is quite cliché and can be challenging to pull off. You'll have to stop the elevators and listen to the alarm which can really break the mood.

BEST POSITION Dancer or Standing Doggy Style

PROS There's just something about fooling around in an elevator that gets us all worked up.

CONS Getting interrupted every time the elevator reaches a new floor and alarm bells going off if you choose to stop between floors.

189. In the Broom Closet of Any Public Building

All public buildings have broom closets, supply closets, and maintenance closets. Make a challenge for yourselves to find one in each public building you enter and enjoy a quickie along the way.

BEST POSITION Dancer or Bodyguard

PROS You can make a really fun game out of this.

CONS Your clothes will be disheveled everywhere you go, if you play the game right.

190. In Your Car

There's something a little juvenile about having sex in the car. There are many places that you can meet for an afternoon tryst or a lunch break like the local park, in the office parking garage, or even your own driveway.

BEST POSITION Game's On or Deck Chair

PROS The car is my favorite place for quickies because you have more control of the environment and you can freshen up before you get out of the car.

CONS Security cameras and parking garage security on patrol can leave you feeling a little exposed.

191. Between Two Parked Cars in a Parking Lot

Come on, you've seen other people doing this outside of a dance club. If they can do it, so can you!

BEST POSITION Standing Oral or Standing Doggy Style

PROS It's dark and no one's watching. If they are, it's doubtful they'll care, unless it's their car.

CONS It's still public sex, so you can get arrested.

192. In Your Friend's Car—the One Who Gave You a Ride to the Party

Don't have your own car with you at the party? Just tell Joe that you forgot something in the car. He'll be happy to give you the keys and you can get freaky in the back seat.

BEST POSITION Deck Chair or Deep Stick

PROS No one will even miss you—at least for the first ten minutes.

CONS You may fog up the windows a bit.

193. In the Dark Alley Behind Your Favorite Club or Restaurant

If you're looking for some raw sex, sneak out the back door of the restaurant or club for a quickie in the back alley.

BEST POSITION Standing Oral or Dancer

PROS It's very spontaneous and primal.

CONS This is typically where they keep the garbage so the smell can be a bit rank.

194. In the Foyer as Soon as You Get Home

This is another one of my favorite places for a quickie. It's very sensual to rush in the door ripping one another's clothes off and landing against the wall for a rough, passionate quickie.

BEST POSITION Dancer or Standing Oral

PROS It's passionate and aggressive.

CONS There's little time for foreplay, but hopefully you've been teasing each other all the way home.

195. In the Laundry Room of an Apartment Building

Live in an apartment building or dorm with a community laundry room? Do your laundry together late at night and enjoy a quickie on the washer or in a chair.

BEST POSITION Lap Dance or Standing Doggy Style

PROS Laundry rooms are typically pretty empty late at night, so you should have some privacy.

CONS You have to stay up late to do your laundry.

196. In the Locker Room after the Game

What a great way to celebrate a big win than with a quickie in the locker room after the game. You can step into the shower or behind the lockers.

BEST POSITION Dancer or Standing Doggy Style

PROS Your adrenaline will be very high so you'll be incredibly aroused.

CONS The rest of the team will also be in the locker room, but they may not mind your impromptu celebration.

197. In the Restroom of Your Favorite Restaurant

This one's so easy to do everyone should try it at least once. Pick a smaller restaurant with a single bathroom, not the ones with stalls, and go into together for a quickie. It can be an appetizer or dessert!

BEST POSITION Mastery or Standing Doggy Style

PROS No one will say anything to you. The most you'll get is an odd look from the person waiting in line behind you.

CONS Once again, it's a public restroom, so be wary of what surfaces you touch with your various body parts.

198. In the Porta-Potty at an Outdoor Concert

This one made the list, but some of you might say "eeww!" If you must have sex in a porta-potty, just don't touch anything and definitely try to keep the thing from rocking back and forth.

BEST POSITION Dancer or Mastery

PROS None—but sometimes you just got to do what you got to do.

CONS This is just a nasty environment.

199. In the Trees after Ziplining

Ziplining is the sport of soaring high above the ground while your body is secured in a harness and attached to an overhead cable. The cable normally built high over scenic areas such as ravines and jungles. It gives you an incredibly huge rush. Although you probably can't have sex while ziplining, a pit stop in the trees will keep that rush going.

BEST POSITION Dancer or Missionary

PROS What's better than zipping through trees and then getting sexual afterward? What an incredible high!

CONS Being in the woods offers its fair share of bugs, sticks, and dirt, naked or not.

200. In the Restroom of a Commuter Train

Make the ride home from work a little more exciting. If you don't work together, surprise your partner with a chance encounter on the train and then sneak off to the restroom for a quickie.

BEST POSITION Dancer or Bodyguard

PROS It's very spontaneous and exciting.

CONS It's a very small, cramped space.

201. In the Sleigh That Takes You Through the Haunted House Ride

What a great opportunity to snuggle and get close. No one will say anything if you're in his lap. Just pretend to be frightened and let him be the strong, fearless man that you know he is.

BEST POSITION Mastery or Lap Dance

PROS It'll be dark so no one will notice what you're doing.

CONS Make sure that your moaning blends in with the moaning from the haunted house.

202. Under a Deserted Pier at the Beach

Next time you're taking a romantic stroll on the beach, stop for a quickie under the pier.

BEST POSITION Dancer or Standing Doggy Style

PROS It's dark and quiet. Chances are you'll go completely undisturbed.

CONS Make sure to be aware of your surroundings because you may not be alone under the pier.

203. In the Stairwell of an Apartment Building

Stairwells are a great place for a quickie, especially if you can find one that's not very busy. You can lean up against the wall, sit on the steps, or lean over the railing. Just use your imagination.

BEST POSITION Dancer or Standing Doggy Style

PROS Let's face it; even though we know better, most of us still take the elevator, not the stairs.

CONS Most stairwells are not very clean places, and you may not be the only ones who decide to take the stairs.

204. In Your New House That's Still Under Construction

Christen your new house by having a quickie before they even get all the walls up. You can do it again after they put down the carpet!

BEST POSITION Dancer or Standing Doggy Style

PROS It's your house. What can anyone really say?

CONS Be careful of nails, splinters, and other construction site obstacles.

205. In the Master Bedroom at Your Best Friend's Party

Enjoy a quickie in your best friend's Master Bedroom. He/She won't mind, simply excuse yourselves to the restroom and take a detour to the bedroom for a quick romp.

BEST POSITION Missionary or Cowgirl

PROS It just feels a little naughty to have sex on your best friend's bed.

CONS Your best friend may not approve of you using the master bedroom for extracurricular activities.

206. In an Airport Restroom During a Layover

Put a new spin on the "mile-high club" and have a quickie in the airport restroom before you catch your next flight out. Slip into a stall together and use the toilets in the stalls for leverage.

BEST POSITION Mastery or Standing Doggy Style

PROS It's a terrific way to kill the time between flights.

CONS Public restrooms are loaded with bacteria. Be careful where you put what.

207. On a Pool Table in an Old-Fashioned Honky-Tonk (Bar)

The pool table is a great place for a quickie. Just bend her over the table or sit her on top and get to it. You get the idea.

BEST POSITION Deck Chair or Deep Impact

PROS The felt on the pool table is soft, not padded, but soft.

CONS Be careful not to get any unintended fluids on the felt—it may not come out—and watch out for unexpected bystanders.

208. The Bathroom of a Bowling Alley

If you haven't noticed already, restrooms, while not the cleanest places, are excellent places for a quickie.

BEST POSITION Dancer or Standing Doggy Style

PROS It's a great way to celebrate a new high score.

CONS As with all bathrooms, it's dirty so watch where you touch.

209. The Outdoor Restroom of a Gas Station

Stop in at an old-fashioned gas station for a refill. While they're washing your windows, you can get the key to the bathroom and run in for a quickie.

BEST POSITION Dancer or Standing Doggy Style

PROS It'll be an adventure.

CONS These are some of the absolute nastiest restrooms, but maybe you'll get lucky and it's been recently cleaned.

210. In the Restroom of a Convenience Store

Run into the store for a soda, some chips, and a quickie in the bathroom.

BEST POSITION Dancer or Standing Doggy Style

PROS Convenience stores were designed to be "quick."

CONS It's a restroom.

211. Up Against Any Wall in Your House

We've already talked about the foyer being a great place for a quickie, but in reality, any wall or counter top is fair game. Try them all and see what you like best.

BEST POSITION Dancer or Bodyguard

PROS You'll have sex in every room in your house. (You haven't done this already?)

CONS Be careful not to knock off any family photos.

212. While Pretending to Be Interested in a Ridiculously Expensive House You Can't Afford

Most expensive homes are shown by appointment only, but even the million-dollar houses have open houses on Sundays. With a house that large, there are tons of places to hide for quickie.

BEST POSITION Dancer or Standing Doggy Style

PROS It's a great opportunity for some dream building—imagine that this is your house.

CONS Open houses for the nicer homes can be pretty busy, but there are still many places to hide.

213. While Checking Out Guest Rooms at a Prospective Hotel

When you stay at a new hotel, make it a point to check a few different guest rooms and a few different views. If the hotel staff is busy, they'll just give you the keys and tell you which rooms are available. Are you starting to see how you can really have some fun with this?

BEST POSITION Missionary or Cowgirl

PROS They won't suspect anything for twenty minutes.

CONS Make sure to lock the door to avoid unwanted interruptions.

CHAPTER 4

THE
BACK ROW

Remember when you were a teenager, or younger, and always wanted to sit in the back row so that you could goof off or make out? Guess what, you can regain that sense of adventure regardless of your age.

214. In the Back Row of a Local Play

Stage a good time for your lover by making love at a play.

BEST POSITION Lap Dance or Game's On

PROS What an incredible way to spice up a boring play! Even if the play is good, it's a great way to add excitement to your night.

CONS You may get thrown out.

215. In the Back Row of a Loud Symphony

The back row is alive with the sound of music and the moans of your partner. Make your own music and see how loud you can get without anyone hearing you!

BEST POSITION Lap Dance or Game's On

PROS Music moves the soul.

CONS You may get thrown out.

216. In the Back Row of a Magic Show

Make your own magic at a magic show! It's definitely a fun and new way to get your freak on with your partner and see what you can make disappear!

Depending on the magic show and whether it's stadium seating or tables, you can really get creative with this one.

BEST POSITION Lap Dance or Game's On

PROS It's normally very dark at magic shows.

CONS You'll miss part of the show.

217. In the Back Row of a Movie

The best time for this one is Tuesday around 2 P.M. The movie theater is less crowded and you're less likely to be noticed by anyone who cares.

BEST POSITION Lap Dance or Game's On

PROS The Lap Dance position allows you to both continue watching the movie—that's if you still care about the movie.

CONS You may get thrown out of the theater or arrested by vice cops (we've all seen *Miami Vice*, right?) hoping to have the back of the theater to themselves.

218. In the Back Row of a Lecture on Quantum Physics

Pass the time by having some fun with your partner—assuming you can get them to the lecture in the first place.

BEST POSITION Game's On or Manual Stimulation

PROS Anyone who really cares about the lecture is sitting toward the front—everyone else is comatose.

CONS It's very public so you'll have to limit yourselves to oral or manual action.

219. In the Back Row of a Vegas Show

When those Vegas dancers start their show, you can start one of your own. You might not be in the bright lights, but for what you're doing, that may not be such a bad thing.

BEST POSITION Lap Dance or Game's On

PROS It's normal for people to let go in Vegas, so you may not even get a second glance from those sitting around you.

CONS Getting caught and thrown out of Vegas isn't as bad as it sounds. It happens all the time!

220. In the Back Row of an IMAX Theater

Bigger is better, or so they say. Imagine the fun of sex at the movies with a bigger screen and a huge theater! Sex on a real roller coaster is next to impossible so the IMAX is the next best thing.

BEST POSITION Lap Dance or Game's On

PROS Added adrenalin from the Imax experience.

CONS Same cons as going to a regular movie theater—you could get caught and thrown out.

221. In the Highest Row of a "Insert Your Favorite Sport Here" Game

Okay, this one's for all of you sports fans out there. Why not make your favorite sporting event even better? If you're in the top row, no one cares what you're doing because they're watching the game!

BEST POSITION Lap Dance or Game's On

PROS It gives you something to do while your partner watches the game.

CONS What if he or she is more interested in the game than you?

222. In the Highest Row of a Concert

Concerts are a great place to let go and have a good time. Especially at concerts, the top rows are incredibly dark and most of the people at that level will be too drunk or stoned to pay you much mind.

BEST POSITION Lap Dance or Game's On

PROS It's very dark and loud—so you can feel free to moan and scream all you want.

CONS Concert venues can have very steep seating, so be careful not to fall forward.

CHAPTER 5

IN A
DARK CORNER

Darks corners are everywhere if you just pay attention, and every dark corner is an opportunity for you to grow the passion in your relationship.

223. In the Back Corner of Your Favorite Museum

Next time you're enjoying a cultural date, take a few minutes to enjoy each other as well.

BEST POSITION Dancer or Standing Doggy Style

PROS It's a good way to take some of the stuffiness out of your museum tour.

CONS Try not to break any priceless artifacts.

224. In a Dark Corner of a Disco

Dance clubs have plenty of dark corners to have some sexy fun.

BEST POSITION Dancer or Bodyguard

PROS It's dark and music is thumpin'.

CONS Standing too close to the speakers can leave your ears ringing for days.

225. In a Dark Corner of a Swank Night Club

If you're in Portland, Maine, you have to stop into 51 Wharf on a Saturday night. You will find a wide selection of fine food and nightlife.

BEST POSITION Dancer or Game's On

PROS It seems that you can get away with more in the nicer clubs. They're all about customer service.

CONS Bouncers can make your visit short lived.

226. In the Dark Corner of an Art Gallery

Art is used as an appreciation of beauty. Contribute in your own way.

BEST POSITION Dancer or Bodyguard

PROS This is a right-brained activity, so you can feel free to get creative.

CONS There'll be security cameras and guards.

227. In a Dark Corner of the Bingo Hall

Let your partner know they've hit the right spot than by yelling, "Bingo!"

BEST POSITION Game's On or Manual Stimulation

PROS Bingo isn't just fun for the elderly!

CONS Bingo halls seem to be the last converters to the idea of a nonsmoking venue, but they're catching up.

228. In a Dark Corner of the Bowling Alley

If you're good, you can strike it lucky here.

BEST POSITION Dancer or Standing Oral

PROS You can make a game of it—different pin combinations, mean different sex acts.

CONS It's possible to get kicked out.

229. In a Dark Corner of the Coffee House

You can either stand up in a corner or possibly do it sitting, or you may have to fall back on the tried-and-true restroom break.

BEST POSITION Dancer or Standing Doggy Style

PROS Caffeine is a stimulant so you won't get tired.

CONS Coffee houses are not set up for privacy, so you may have to look around to find one that's cozy.

230. In a Dark Corner of a Wine Bar

Wine bars are typically cozier than coffee houses. Look around to find one that is set up in a way to give you some privacy.

BEST POSITION Dancer or Standing Doggy Style

PROS Wine can relax the mood.

CONS It's still a public place.

231. In a Dark Corner of a Swinger Club

A swinger club is basically one big dark corner. Pick a shadow and enjoy!

BEST POSITION Standing Oral or Dancer

PROS Everyone there wants you to enjoy yourself.

CONS Another couple may want to join you. That's only a con if you don't want them to.

232. In a Dark Corner of a Hookah Lounge

Hookah lounges are very laid back with pillows on the floor and very cozy tables. It's also typically very dark so you can get away with more.

BEST POSITION Game's On or Spoons

PROS Hookah smoke is supposed to be better than straight tobacco smoke because it's filtered through water.

CONS It's still smoke, so use with moderation.

233. In a Corner of the Reptile House at the Zoo

Get primal in the reptile house. Look for a room where they're installing a new exhibit, or look for a dark hallway like where you might find a fire exit.

BEST POSITION Dancer or Standing Doggy Style

PROS It's dark and cool on a hot summer day.

CONS There's a probability of kids running around.

234. At a Gym in an Unused Aerobics Room

Get a workout after your workout!

BEST POSITION Bodyguard or Dancer

PROS It's hard to dread the gym when there is hot sex!

CONS If you get caught you may lose your membership.

CHAPTER 6

BEST PLACES TO HAVE SEX WHILE SHOPPING

You can even turn a day of shopping into an erotic adventure. Some of these places will surprise you, others will shock you, and some will make you say "Why didn't I think of that?" Find the ones that resonate with you and give them a try.

235. While Apartment Hunting

Many times you'll get to look at an apartment on your own without the realtor peering over your shoulder. Take advantage of it! Have sex on the floor, on the kitchen counter, or even on the balcony!

BEST POSITION Anything goes!

PROS You can rate if the apartment is right for you based on how good the sex is!

CONS Some apartment landlords won't leave you alone long enough to talk about the place or do anything else.

236. While You're Out Test Driving a New Car

The car is not the only thing going for a test ride. Get freaky with your partner in the back seat, the front seat, or even on the hood of the car. The salesperson may want to go with you the first time, but if you come back for a second or third test drive, they'll usually let you take the car on your own. Sometimes they'll even let you keep it overnight.

BEST POSITION Mastery or Deck Chair

PROS The car company will have no idea what happened but you will!

CONS Don't do any physical damage to the car and you're in the clear.

237. In a New Downtown Loft That's for Sale

The acoustics in a loft are really cool. Find one with a great view and pretend to be a prospective buyer. See if you can get a few minutes alone to discuss how you both feel about it. Make love right in front of the windows.

BEST POSITION Dancer or Bodyguard

PROS You get to see a really awesome downtown loft.

CONS Most realtors are very aggressive and may not leave you alone for very long.

238. In a Public Restroom at Your Local Department Store

Slip into the handicap stall together for a quickie. While it's a public restroom, there's still some legal question if it's public indecency because of the expected privacy in the stall. Check with an attorney to be sure.

BEST POSITION Mastery or Bodyguard

PROS It's a great break from a long day of shopping.

CONS It's a public bathroom. Don't touch anything.

239. Behind the Clothing Rack in a Messy Department Store

This works well in a store where the clothes are crammed on the racks rather than a luxury store where the clothes are hung for presentation.

BEST POSITION Doggy Style and Dancer

PROS It's a great way to make a trip to the outlet stores more fun.

CONS Oddly enough, the outlet stores are more prudish about what you can get away with. They won't even let you go in the dressing rooms together.

240. In the Family Restroom at the Mall

Tired of shopping? Take a break for a quickie in the family restroom. It's way more private than the his and her bathrooms. You don't really think you're the first one to do this do you?

BEST POSITION Mastery or Standing Doggy Style

PROS It's roomy and you can lock the door. Plus, you can freshen up before you go.

CONS It's a public bathroom so you may want to take minute to wipe down any surfaces.

241. Department Store Dressing Room

Go to Saks 5th Avenue or Neiman Marcus, as the nicer stores don't really question what you're doing in the dressing room and are more likely to give you the privacy you desire. They will likely offer you water, coffee, and a snack, plus the dressing rooms are much nicer!

BEST POSITION Dancer or Standing Doggy Style

PROS Very spontaneous with lots of adrenaline because you're doing something you "shouldn't."

CONS Keep spanking to a minimum as it may result in unwanted attention.

242. In the VIP Lounge at a Fancy Jewelry Store

Some of the nicer jewelry stores have a "VIP" lounge where you can have coffee and even a small snack.

BEST POSITION Mastery or Lap Dance

PROS These lounges are not normally very busy, so you may just have the room to yourself.

CONS Sometimes these rooms are reserved for paying, regular customers.

243. In a Display Shower at the Home Improvement Store

There's something sexy about having sex in the shower, but there's something even kinkier about having sex in a display shower that is open to everyone's view!

BEST POSITION Dancer or Bodyguard

PROS A trip to the home improvement store to pick up nails never has to be boring again!

CONS This is a very public place to have sex. You'll probably get caught and thrown out.

244. On the Exercise Equipment at a Department Store

Make sex on an exercise bench a public affair. Try this at a department store rather than fitness store because the exercise equipment at a store like Sears is off in a corner somewhere.

BEST POSITION Cowgirl or Dancer

PROS It's a great release of your inhibitions.

CONS It's also a great way to get thrown out of the store and even arrested.

245. In a Show Camper at a Sports Store

When you make your way to the sports store, you can ask your partner to check out that camper you've always had your eye on. Get a good idea of how well you like it by trying it out first!

BEST POSITION Missionary or Doggy Style

PROS It's public and private at the same time! It's a great way to sneak a quickie.

CONS Don't tip the camper over and don't draw attention to yourself by making too much noise.

246. In a $250,000 Tour Bus at a Travel Show

Have you seen these things? They're absolute luxury on wheels. Step inside and go into the bedroom for a quickie.

BEST POSITION Missionary or cowgirl

PROS Another dream-building opportunity—imagine that it's your bus and you're traveling the country.

CONS Even though these buses are quite luxurious, the space is still very small.

247. In a Log-Home Demo

Log homes are big, beautiful, and full of great places to have sex. Maybe you don't own your own log home, but a demo will give you a way to experience it all without the huge price tag.

BEST POSITION Missionary or Doggy Style

PROS Spending a Saturday afternoon admiring log homes and each other's bodies is a great way to combat boredom.

CONS You may decide to buy a log home even it it's not in the budget.

248. In a Mobile-Home Demo

Stop at a mobile home demo on a road trip and have someone show you around. When they leave, it's time to get freaky!

BEST POSITION Missionary or Doggy Style

PROS What a great way to take a break on a long road trip.

CONS If you get a pushy salesperson, they may linger—politely tell them you'd like a few minutes to talk to each other and then you can get busy.

249. In a Show Car in the Middle of the Mall

Slip in and take a ride to the erotic. This makes for a good chance to get nasty in the backseat of some nice cars. Wait until just before closing time so that the mall won't be so crowded.

BEST POSITION Missionary or Deck Chair

PROS The great thing about mall show cars is that most of them have very dark tinted windows.

CONS Some people want to press their faces close and peer inside, giving them a full view of what is going on in there!

250. In a Show Tent at a Sports Store

If you don't like camping outdoors, you can still take a little trip into the rugged side of things by "camping" out for a quickie in a show tent.

BEST POSITION Missionary or Doggy Style

PROS It feels like being in a clubhouse—you know like the ones you used to make as a kid.

CONS You never know if someone is going to want to look at the inside of the tent while you're still in there.

251. In an Armchair at the Furniture Store

If you're an exhibitionist, you'll definitely get a kick out of having sex on a display chair at the furniture store. While you're at it, try the couch too! You definitely run the risk of being caught and possibly being charged for the furniture (and for indecent exposure).

BEST POSITION Mastery or Lap Dance

PROS Most furniture stores are pretty empty, so you should be able to pull this one off if you wear easy access clothing.

CONS The salesperson will not be happy if you get caught.

252. On Top of a Washer or Dryer at the Department Store

Again, go to a store where appliances are not the main thing they sell. That way, there'll be fewer people in the appliance section of the store.

BEST POSITION Delight or Standing Doggy Style

PROS You can decide if you like the washer and dryer based on the height.

CONS Once again, the salespeople will not be happy if they catch you in the act.

253. On a Sample Bed in a Mattress Store

Take a mattress for a test ride!

BEST POSITION Missionary or Delight

PROS What a great way to test-drive a mattress!

CONS If you try real sex, you could get into real trouble, so make sure to be very discreet.

254. At the Santa Claus Photo Area at the Mall

When the mall is closing, catch a quickie after Santa has left his post.

BEST POSITION Missionary or Dancer

PROS It will be a Christmas memory you'll never forget.

CONS Make sure that if you get caught, it's by the security guard and not children looking for a couple of elves.

255. In the Dressing Room at a Lingerie Store

Most lingerie stores will let you go both into the dressing room.

BEST POSITION Dancer or Standing Doggy Style

PROS There's nothing more arousing than trying on lingerie—together.

CONS The salespeople tend to hover nearby.

256. At the Easter Bunny Photo Area at the Mall

Slip behind an Easter display after hours and get nice and naughty!

BEST POSITION Missionary or Dancer

PROS You can play hide the "Easter egg."

CONS There is a chance of getting caught, but less if you do it after the Easter Bunny has retired for the night.

CHAPTER 7

EXHIBITIONIST EXTREME

Some of us just love to be center stage in every area of our lives including sex. If this sounds like you, then this chapter is for you!

257. On the Big Screen at a Sporting Event

The next time you're at a baseball game and they're putting all of the romantic kisses on the big screen, give them some shock value by doing more than kissing.

BEST POSITION Standing Oral or Standing Doggy Style

PROS Every eye will be on you.

CONS You'll likely be kicked out of the stadium but it'll be worth it.

258. On National TV

Get creative and find a way to be on national TV. Try something like standing outside of the *Good Morning America* studios or in the background of a live news event.

BEST POSITION Standing Oral or Standing Doggy Style

PROS You'll be on national TV.

CONS If it's not a truly live event, they'll just edit you out, so make sure that it's really live.

259. While Waiting in Line—Anywhere

Bring out the true exhibitionist in you by fondling each other next time you're waiting in line—anywhere. The grocery store, the bank, for concert tickets, etc. Be creative.

BEST POSITION Manual Stimulation or Dancer

PROS You can be as crazy or mild as you like.

CONS If you get too adventurous, you'll get kicked out of line (not get your tickets) and maybe even arrested.

260. In the Produce Aisle of the Grocery Store

Get freaky in the produce aisle next time you're doing some late-night shopping.

BEST POSITION Standing Doggy Style or Bodyguard

PROS Yet another chance to play with your inner exhibitionist.

CONS You may get kicked out of the store—permanently, so don't try this at your favorite shopping spot.

261. Standing on Any Street Corner

Give the traffic control guys a cheap thrill by having sex on a street corner. With all the cameras these days, you can bet someone will be watching. The question is will they turn you in or not?

BEST POSITION Dancer or Bodyguard

PROS It's very freeing.

CONS You can be arrested.

262. While Lounging at the Hotel Pool in the Middle of the Afternoon

Take a break from sunbathing and get a little freaky on the lounge chair.

BEST POSITION Cowgirl or Deck Chair

PROS Nicer hotels have really comfy lounge chairs.

CONS Make sure that the lounge chair will support your weight to avoid turning a sexy display into an embarrassing moment.

263. On Top of the Baggage Claim Carousel at the Airport

You'll have to act fast to get very far with this one, but it's worth a try!

BEST POSITION Doggy Style or Missionary

PROS You'll be getting it on while the rest of the passengers watch.

CONS Airport security will be there in less than three minutes.

264. On the Shuttle to the Airport

Make the shuttle ride to the airport more interesting for you and the other passengers.

BEST POSITION Mastery or Bodyguard

PROS If the shuttle is really crowded (standing room only), the person next to you may just think it's the swaying and rocking ride of the shuttle.

CONS If the driver gets offended, you may be walking to the airport.

265. Standing on a Balcony at Mardi Gras

This is one of the few places in America where this sort of thing is celebrated! So what are you waiting for?

BEST POSITION Bodyguard or Standing Doggy Style

PROS You'll get lots of beads!

CONS What'll you do with all those beads?

266. On Stage at a Rock Concert

Most people run on stage to grab someone in the band. You can run up on stage and start making a little music of your own.

BEST POSITION Standing Doggy Style or Deep Stick

PROS You may get a standing ovation.

CONS Or you may get arrested.

267. On the Hood of a Ferrari on the Showroom Floor

It doesn't get more sexy and forbidden than this. Your time will likely be very limited here as well, so don't hesitate; just do it!

BEST POSITION Butterfly or Delight

PROS You definitely get bragging rights for this one.

CONS If you scratch it, you buy it.

268. A Live Webcast from Your Bedroom

This one will require some research and energy but could end up not only being fun but also paying well. There are even online services that will pay you to have people watch you and your lover making love.

BEST POSITION Spread Eagle or Atten Hut

PROS Excitement of knowing literally millions of people could be watching you and your lover.

CONS There may be legal limits where you live or where it's being broadcast. Plus your kids or parents could end up seeing you.

269. Huge Public Fountain

You've probably seen a huge fountain before and just wish you could jump in, especially on a hot day or sultry summer evening. Ignore your inhibitions and get frisky with your partner while you both are getting wet.

BEST POSITION Dancer or Bodyguard

PROS It's sexy, it's fun, and it's incredibly refreshing. What is not to love?

CONS It's a public fountain, so you run the real risk of getting arrested.

270. Storefront Window after Hours

Let the exhibitionist in you run wild. Have sex in the storefront window and see if the people passing by really see what you're doing. They may not even notice or you may have an audience of 100.

BEST POSITION Standing Oral or Bodyguard

PROS It's like being on stage.

CONS If you work at the store, you may get fired.

271. Any Enclosed Bus Stop

Enjoy your time while waiting for the bus. An enclosed bus stop gives you a little more freedom than an open bus stop to really get freaky.

BEST POSITION Lap Dance or Mastery

PROS It's a public place that's not too public—great for the first time exhibitionist.

CONS Bus stops are not the cleanest places in the world.

272. At an Open Bus Stop

The challenge is to have sex without anyone knowing you're having sex. Wearing a loose-fitting skirt is always a good option to avoid getting caught.

BEST POSITION Lap Dance or Game's On

PROS It's a place to bring out your inner exhibitionist.

CONS The chance for getting arrested is high.

273. On the Balcony of Your Hotel Room

You can make it more public by having sex in full view or less public by hiding under a blanket on the lounge chair.

BEST POSITION Standing Doggy Style or Cowgirl

PROS You get to control your level of public exposure.

CONS The neighbors may complain but it's more likely that they'll run for their binoculars.

274. On a Park Bench

Park benches are a great place to cuddle and kiss, or take it all the way.

BEST POSITION Lap Dance or Game's On

PROS This is a romantic way to have public sex.

CONS Private, out-of-the-way park benches may not be in the safest areas, so be aware of your surroundings.

275. Behind the Bushes at a Public Park

Can't find a bench that's private enough? Then sneak behind the bushes.

BEST POSITION Missionary or Spread Eagle

PROS It feels very juvenile and sneaky.

CONS Rocks, sticks, and bugs—bring a blanket.

276. Cybersex with a Live Web Cam

Plug in your web cams and start with steamy chatting. Gradually move into some flashes on the cam and just see where it goes from there.

BEST POSITION Anything goes!

PROS It's a terrific way to release your inhibitions.

CONS This one is limited to masturbation unless you invite a friend.

277. In the Living Room with the Windows Open

Having the windows open adds adventure, and don't worry, it's highly unlikely that anyone can see you from the street.

BEST POSITION Cowgirl or Standing Doggy Style

PROS It's a safe way to explore your exhibitionist side.

CONS The neighbors may disapprove, if you're loud.

278. In a Public Pool

Having sex in a public pool is very risky and titillating.

BEST POSITION Bodyguard or modified Drill (man standing and girl has legs wrapped around his waist)

PROS Swimsuits are easy on, easy off!

CONS Water is not a lubricant—put on a silicon-based lubricant before you get in the pool and use extra.

279. Diving Board of Your Neighbor's Pool

Don't have a diving board? No problem—use your neighbor's diving board.

BEST POSITION Cowgirl or Game's On

PROS It's unlikely they'll call the cops.

CONS Diving boards are typically hard and rough so bring a towel to add some cushioning.

CHAPTER 8

BEST PUBLIC PLACES TO HAVE SEX

Maybe you're an exhibitionist and are thrilled at the idea of others watching you have sex. Or maybe you are just curious and want to explore the idea of sex in public to see if you can get away with it. Either way, this section is for you. If you're going to try the places in this section, just remember that public sex is considered indecent exposure and you may be ticketed or even arrested if caught, so proceed with caution.

280. At a College Bonfire

It was very sad when the Texas Aggie bonfire collapsed for many reasons, including the loss of life and the end of a tradition. While you may not be able to find a bonfire like that anywhere, it's still a tradition at a lot of other schools and one that should not be missed.

BEST POSITION Missionary or Dancer

PROS The fire and heat from a large bonfire brings our primal energies to life.

CONS Don't get too close to the bonfire or you may get burned.

281. At a PTA Meeting

Another boring Parent Teacher Association meeting? Find an empty classroom and have a quickie.

BEST POSITION Mastery or Dancer

PROS The meeting will go much faster.

CONS You may get kicked out of the PTA and have to explain why to your children.

282. In the Hot Tub at a Luxury Spa

Enjoy the hot tub at a luxury spa—together. The atmosphere is so serene and calming that you'll literally meld together.

BEST POSITION Mastery or Delight

PROS You can get a massage when you're done.

CONS You may knock over your peach iced tea.

283. In the Relaxation Room at the Spa

While you're waiting for your spa treatment to begin, you can enjoy some casual foreplay and more.

BEST POSITION Manual Stimulation or Game's On

PROS It's a very romantic and peaceful setting.

CONS It's a shame to mess up the energy by getting too rowdy, so keep it slow and sensual.

284. In a Wave Pool at a Water Park

If you can't have the real ocean, try a wave pool! Ride the wave with your partner's body underneath yours! You'll get a kick out of the motion of the ocean in conjunction with the motion of your bodies.

BEST POSITION Standing Doggy Style or Bodyguard

PROS The public nature of a wave pool will thrill even the most daring couples.

CONS It can be extremely difficult to avoid crowds of parents and children.

285. In the Bushes at Six Flags

There are dark corners and bushes and trails all over Six Flags. Use them to your advantage.

BEST POSITION Dancer or Bodyguard

PROS Anytime the urge strikes you, there's probably a corner to duck around.

CONS There's a very high kid density, so beware of who is watching you.

286. During an Air-Conditioned Show at Six Flags

This works really well in the shows where you get to sit on the floor. Pick a spot in the back and enjoy.

BEST POSITION Spoons or Lotus

PROS If you go during the week, it's not very crowded.

CONS You still run the risk of being seen by children or their parents, so please be respectful of others who may be sitting around you.

287. On a Virtual Roller Coaster Ride at Six Flags

Enjoy one of those IMAX-like roller coaster rides—only enjoy it with your partner in your lap. Pick one of the stationary rides for this one rather than the ones that actually move around.

BEST POSITION Lap Dance or Manual Stimulation

PROS It's normally pretty dark and you'll get the thrill of the coaster without the rough ride.

CONS If you're one who suffers from motion sickness or vertigo, this may not the best choice for you.

288. On a Hand-Carved Carousel Ride

Enjoy a ride on an antique carousel ride. Look for one that's not very busy and will let you ride together. For many of these public places, having her wear a longer loose skirt really helps to conceal what you're doing. It may not be fashionable, but that's not what we're going for here.

BEST POSITION Mastery or Lap Dance

PROS You can go up and down with the horses.

CONS It may be challenging to ride together. If they won't let you sit on a horse together, ride in one of the booth seats and enjoy some manual action.

289. While Playing Mini Golf

How about playing a game of strip golf? Every time you lose the hole or your partner gets a hole in one, you take off an article of clothing. When you're out of clothes, you have to perform sexual favors.

BEST POSITION Missionary or Dancer

PROS Mini golf can be boring and this is an incredible way to make it more fun.

CONS Obviously you'll have to reserve the course for a private party.

290. At a Dog Show

Put your head up high and your tail out. Do it like the dogs do!

BEST POSITION Doggy Style or Standing Doggy Style

PROS You get to check out each other and some really cool dogs at the same time.

CONS It's a public place and not everyone may appreciate your animal instincts.

291. At a Dog Park

Hide in the bushes and do it like the REAL dogs do. Nothing pretentious here.

BEST POSITION Doggy Style or Standing Doggy Style

PROS There are more bushes and places to hide.

CONS Poop—lots and lots of poop.

292. While Skinning Dipping at the Lake

This is probably the most common place where people have public sex.

BEST POSITION Delight or Bodyguard

PROS Everyone has sex at the lake so it's no big deal.

CONS Some lakes can be "less than sanitary" so be careful where you swim and avoid areas with stagnant water.

293. At Your Neighborhood "National Night Out" Party

National Night Out is unique crime/drug prevention event celebrated in neighborhoods across the country. Basically, everyone in the neighborhood gets together for a block party or cookout. Enjoy your own version of community spirit by sneaking away for a quick romp with your partner.

BEST POSITION Dancer or Bodyguard

PROS These events are held in the community park or in the middle of the street, so there are plenty of places to sneak away for a quick romp—behind a tree, around the side of the house, or even in the pool.

CONS If your neighbors catch you, you may not be invited back next year.

294. In a Sculpture Garden

Enjoy posing with the statues. Make some sexual statues of your own.

BEST POSITION Dancer or Bodyguard

PROS Get creative and have some fun.

CONS Be careful not to damage the sculptures.

295. In the Movie Room at Your Apartment Complex

Newer apartment complexes have incredible movie rooms that no one ever uses!

BEST POSITION Mastery or Missionary

PROS No one ever goes in there so you'll probably be undisturbed.

CONS If you do get caught, you may have to find another place to live—but hopefully you'll get a warning first.

296. In the Club House at Your Apartment Complex

Someone needs to enjoy that huge building that always seems to be empty.

BEST POSITION Mastery or Delight

PROS It's like having your own really cool game room.

CONS It's more public than the movie room.

297. In the Public Kitchen at Your Apartment Complex Clubhouse

Many apartment complexes have a clubhouse with media room, business center, and kitchen. The kitchen is the most public option of the three but why not grab a quickie while you're grabbing a cup of coffee.

BEST POSITION Standing Doggy Style or Bodyguard

PROS There's no better way to wake up.

CONS Other visitors to the kitchen may not be so pleased with the new developments.

298. In a Castle

You don't have to dress like a bar wench, but you can experience a bit of the Renaissance by sneaking into a dark corner of a castle with your partner while on a tour.

BEST POSITION Bodyguard or Standing Oral

PROS You'll feel like a real prince or princess, at least one that is doing the forbidden!

CONS Tour guides can definitely get nosy if they think someone is up to no good.

299. On Top of a Double-Decker Bus

This time you can both be on top. Use the top of a double-decker bus for a load of fun, especially if it's just you and your lover up there.

BEST POSITION Mastery or Lap Dance

PRO What a fun way to make a normal bus ride incredibly exciting and titillating!

CONS You could get banned from the bus but what a story!

300. Next to a Dinosaur or a Caveman Exhibit

Get primal with the dinosaurs. Depending on the exhibit, you may even be able to lie down in the exhibit itself.

BEST POSITION Doggy Style or Rear Entry

PROS It's a great chance to get in touch with your primal side.

CONS Be careful not to damage any real artifacts.

301. In a Show Boat in the Middle of the Mall

Rock the boat with a little bit of lovemaking. The great thing about a show boat in the mall is that you can really enjoy yourself without many people noticing!

BEST POSITION Missionary or Deck Chair

PROS It's a great way to experience public sex in a semi-private setting. If you're ducked down low enough or in a boat with a lower level, it's unlikely you'll be caught.

CONS Don't rock the boat too hard, or it may come loose from its supports and you'll find yourself rolling down the center of the mall.

302. In an Observatory

Observatories contain some of the most technologically advanced ways to view our atmosphere and deep space. Enjoy the view and observe your partner too! You'll never know what you'll find in an observatory, maybe a dark corner or a huge telescope. Use your imagination!

BEST POSITION Lap Dance or Standing Doggy Style

PROS Make learning about the atmosphere and deep space thrilling!

CONS It's easy to get caught, if you mind that sort of thing!

303. In a Bed at the Emergency Room

If you've ever gone to the emergency room with a minor complaint, you know that the wait can be hours and hours. You may have to wait for a bed, but when you get a bed, you'll have to wait even longer!

BEST POSITION Missionary or Spoons

PROS How exciting will it be to have sex in the emergency room?

CONS If you're worried about the people who really need that bed? They got a bed long before you did.

304. In the Foam Pit at Your Local Gymnastics Academy

Jump into the foam pit after hours for some padded fun.

BEST POSITION Doggy Style or Deep Impact

PROS It's very juvenile.

CONS It might be a bit dirty—just imagine what the kids do in there.

305. In a Public Park on a Swing Set

The swing provides hours of entertainment simply because it allows freedom of movement for some acrobatic moments of intense pleasure. You might want to visit the park at night because in broad daylight, it's easy to get spotted.

BEST POSITION Lap Dance or Standing Doggy Style

PROS It's a much cheaper version of a sex swing and it's much stronger than the swing set in your backyard.

CONS It's a public park, so keep your eyes open and beware of your surroundings.

306. In the Projection Booth of the Movie Theater

If you know someone who works at or owns a movie theater, this can be really fun. Have sex during the movie with a few hundred people just a few feet below you.

BEST POSITION Standing Doggy Style or Bodyguard

PROS Have sex, watch the movie, eat some popcorn—sounds like heaven!

CONS Don't get so crazy that you shake the projector.

307. In the Show Room of a Neon Art Gallery

Having sex among all of the glowing art is awesome.

BEST POSITION Anything goes!

PROS The colors and glowing aura can be very erotic.

CONS Getting permission from the artist may be a challenge but can be done.

308. In Santa's Big Chair at the Mall

After Santa goes home, you can sneak into his chair for a Christmas romp.

BEST POSITION Delight or Lap Dance

PROS You get to sit in "Santa's" lap and tell him everything you want for Christmas.

CONS Keep an eye out for Mall Security.

309. Jungle Gym in the Park

Have you ever seen how crazy kids get on a jungle gym? Imagine how much fun it would be with two adults and a randy imagination!

BEST POSITION Standing Doggy Style or Mastery

PROS You can try all kinds of angles and positions.

CONS It's a public park, so be aware of your surroundings.

310. On the Big Slide at the Park

You can have sex on the ladder or at the bottom of the slide,

BEST POSITION Standing Doggy Style or Mastery

PROS You'll feel like a kid again, albeit a naughty one.

CONS Wipe the slide off first or you may get playground sand in all the wrong places.

311. Empty Ice-Skating Rink

You won't have to worry about getting chilly in the middle of the skating rink. Yes, your clothes will be off, but your partner will be keeping you plenty warm!

BEST POSITION Missionary or Deck Chair

PROS Finding an empty ice-skating rink is fairly easy—they seem to have the weirdest hours.

CONS Bring a sleeping bag to lie on; the ice is cold.

312. Empty Subway Car or Bus

Its public, but not so much. Enjoy the long ride home by having some adult fun on the subway. Standing or sitting, it'll be a ride to remember.

BEST POSITION Mastery or Standing Doggy Style

PROS The subways can get pretty empty after rush hour so use it to your advantage.

CONS Many consider the subway to be dangerous late at night. You'll have to decide for yourself.

313. Exam Room at the Vet's Office

While your pet is away from you getting shots or other medical treatment, relieve your stress with your partner in the exam room. It's just as fun as having sex in the doctor's office!

BEST POSITION Doggy Style or Standing Doggy Style

PROS While you run the risk of being caught, your pet probably won't be denied medical attention if you do get busted.

CONS Don't actually lie on the table or floors because animals excrete all kinds of fluids when they get nervous.

314. Old Vehicle at the Museum of Transportation

Going on a tour of a museum of transportation might not sound like a lot of fun, but it can be if you sneak away and get cozy in a train, automobile, or even a plane that is on display.

BEST POSITION Missionary or Mastery

PROS Explore history and your sexuality at the same time.

CONS Be very careful not to damage any of the displays.

315. Unused Room at the Hot Yoga Studio

Slip into an unused room at the hot yoga studio. The rooms are kept between 90–98 degrees with a constant humidity level.

BEST POSITION Lotus or Standing Doggy Style (If you're really feeling adventurous, make it a "downward-facing dog.")

PROS It'll be like having sex in a sauna without getting overheated.

CONS If you get caught you may lose your membership.

316. At a Public Gym in the Locker Room

While less private than an empty exercise or yoga room, you can slip into a shower for some extended play or just pick a time when the locker room is empty for a quickie.

BEST POSITION Dancer or Mastery

PROS It's hard to dread the gym when you have a hot sex session to look forward to!

CONS You're more likely to get caught here, because there are always people coming in and out of the locker room.

317. On the Ninth Hole after a Dance at a Very Swank Private Golf Club

Let go of your inhibitions by rolling in the grass in your tuxedo and evening gown.

BEST POSITION Missionary or Riding the Face

PROS As far as sex in the grass goes, it doesn't get any softer than the grass on a golf green.

CONS The country club may not appreciate your activities.

318. In Your Neighbor's Backyard

Assuming you're friends with your neighbors, this is a safe way to experiment with public sex. It's not really public, but it feels that way because it's your neighbor's yard.

BEST POSITION Mastery or Standing Doggy Style

PROS Your neighbors will never look at you the same again.

CONS Your neighbors may want to join you—only a con if that's not your thing.

319. In a Hospital Bed

Whether you're staying or visiting, have some fun in an adjustable hospital bed. You can raise and lower the bed, raise the head or foot of the bed. Just think of the cool new positions you can try.

BEST POSITION Deep Stick or Cowgirl

PROS The adjustable bed!

CONS It seems like there's always a nurse running in and out of your room!

320. In a Military Plane at an Air Show

Military planes are incredible, especially cargo planes. Many of them are open to the public for viewing, and you can get in the planes and really have fun.

BEST POSITION Mastery or Standing Doggy Style

PROS You can pretend to join the mile-high club while still on the ground.

CONS Don't get locked in a cockpit or other place with all your clothes off!

321. In a Phone Booth

If you can still find one of those old-fashioned stand-up phone booths, get in and close the doors. If you can't find one of those, look for the private phone booth in an airport or train station.

BEST POSITION Dancer or Bodyguard

PROS It's a great way to dabble with public sex because it's public, yet private at the same time.

CONS You'll have limited space to move around.

322. On a Pirate Ship

Go on a pirate dinner cruise for a fun and different evening out. When the pirate ships are battling, sneak off to a dark corner for a rendezvous.

BEST POSITION Missionary or Standing Doggy Style

PROS It's dark and everyone else is paying attention to the show.

CONS The boat may be pretty crowded.

323. In a Private Box at the Opera

Hate opera? Here's a way to make it more interesting. Many private boxes have seating to view the stage as well as more private seating areas.

BEST POSITION Game's On or Lap Dance

PROS It's a very private place to have sex at a public event.

CONS Cost—as with luxury boxes at sporting events, a private box at the opera will cost you more.

324. At the Public Library Between the Stacks of Books

Visit the public library during "off hours" when it's virtually empty and enjoy some mind-expanding sex.

BEST POSITION Dancer or Standing Oral

PROS It'll be pretty easy to find a quiet spot where you'll be undisturbed.

CONS It's very quiet in the library, so you'll need to be quiet as well. Have you ever noticed how well sound carries in the library?

325. In the Basement of the Public Library

Wander down to the basement where they keep all of the books that are out of circulation. It's a great place to get some privacy, especially later in the evening.

BEST POSITION Dancer or Standing Doggy Style

PROS This is the least busy part of the library.

CONS It's likely very dusty and musty smelling.

326. Behind the Reservation Desk at the Public Library

This is the most fun place to have sex in the library, especially if your partner works behind the desk.

BEST POSITION Game's On or Manual Stimulation

PROS You can tease your partner to no end from behind or under the desk.

CONS You may have to visit the basement on his or her next break.

327. In a Public Sauna

There's something so sexy about being with someone in a sauna, wearing nothing but a skimpy towel and sweat dripping all over your bodies.

BEST POSITION Mastery or Standing Oral

PROS Being naked in a sauna is so refreshing and detoxifying!

CONS It's easy to get overheated in a sauna without having sex. Pay attention to your bodies while getting busy and make sure to drink plenty of water. If you feel overheated, stop and get out!

328. In the VIP Area of a Nightclub

There are always naughty things going on inside of a nightclub, why can't you and your partner cash in on the fun? The VIP area normally has more comfortable seating and is typically in a private area or room.

BEST POSITION Dancer or Bodyguard

PROS It's typically comfortable and private.

CONS You'll have to be connected and fork over some cash to get into the VIP area.

329. At a Christmas Parade

Your location at the actual parade (inside a float or standing in the crowd) will determine if you can have sex or just enjoy a little manual stimulation while you wait for the parade to pass by, but it'll be a fun sexual memory either way.

BEST POSITION Dancer or Manual Stimulation

PROS Christmas memories should not just be about presents and jewelry commercials.

CONS It's a very public place with lots of kids running around so plan accordingly.

330. At Every House on the Parade of Homes

The parade of homes can be a fun way to spend a Saturday afternoon. Make it even more fun by having some sexy fun in every single house!

BEST POSITION Try several!

PROS These are typically very nice homes with lots of rooms where you can sneak away unnoticed.

CONS You may run out of energy before the last house.

331. At the Circus

Don't clown around while you're at the circus. Get down and dirty by making your own little sideshow! Enjoy some hand or oral action in the back row, or even intercourse if you're brave enough.

BEST POSITION Lap Dance or Game's On

PROS It's dark and everyone else will typically be looking up or at least at what's going on in the ring.

CONS If it's a traditional circus, there will be little ones running around. Maybe opt for Cirque du Soleil or something more grown up.

332. At a Comic Book Convention

Dress up as you favorite heroes or villains and really get into character. How about Batman and Cat Woman? Or how about Superman and Lois Lane? Enough of the unrequited love already! It's time that they finally hook up.

BEST POSITION Dancer or Standing Doggy Style

PROS It's a great opportunity for some fantasy role play.

CONS Some costumes are incredibly difficult to get off.

333. At a Craft Show

Craft shows can be incredibly boring if you're not into that sort of thing. So if you find yourself being pulled along to a craft show by your significant other, why not spice things up a bit by sneaking behind a display for a little fun?

BEST POSITION Dancer or Standing Doggy Style

PROS Even craft shows can be fun!

CONS Lots of prudish women running around, so be careful not to get caught.

334. At a Film Festival

Why not get kinky Hollywood style (or Utah style) at the Sundance Film Festival? You don't have to be in the film business to enjoy the sites, the people, and some great sex.

BEST POSITION Dancer or Standing Doggy Style

PROS Park City, Utah, is really beautiful.

CONS There's so much going on that you may not want to stop for sex. Don't forget why you're there!

335. At a Japanese Steak House

Eating at a Japanese steakhouse is just as much a live show as it is dinner. Enjoy some fun under the table or sneak off to the bathroom for a private show.

BEST POSITION Game's On or Standing Doggy Style

PROS Excellent food and entertainment are always a plus.

CONS The layout of the restaurant will make it challenging to do anything at your table. There's always someone there wanting to feed you.

336. At a Lawn Concert

Lawn concerts are the perfect place to enjoy some public sex. Snuggle up under a blanket and enjoy each other and some great music.

BEST POSITION Missionary or Spoons

PROS It's dark and the energy at a concert is amazing.

CONS It's still a public place, so keep you clothes on and don't get too crazy unless you want to miss the rest of the show because you got kicked out.

337. At a Local Community Arboretum

Immerse yourself in exotic plants and lush flowers by getting a little freaky at a local community arboretum. It's the best way to learn about the foliage—up close and personal!

BEST POSITION Missionary or Dancer

PROS Get close to nature without leaving the city.

CONS They often have some very rare plants and flowers. Be careful not to crush them.

338. At a Shipwreck Site

Depending on where you are in the boat, you might be able to sneak away to a hidden supply or utility closet and strip down.

BEST POSITION Dancer or Bodyguard

PROS Get a history lesson and have sex at the same time.

CONS You may be on a cramped tour boat with nowhere to run.

339. At a St. Patrick's Day Parade

Unlike being at a Christmas parade, St. Patrick's Day invokes a spirit of adventure and "let's party." So go ahead paint yourself green from head to toe and really get into the spirit!

BEST POSITION Missionary or Butterfly

PROS No one will recognize you.

CONS Have you ever tried to wash off green body paint?

340. At an Ice Cream Parlor

While there's not much you can do in the waiting area of an ice cream parlor, take your ice cream and your partner into the bathroom for a tasty oral treat.

BEST POSITION Standing Oral or Standing Doggy Style

PROS While you're in the bathroom you can wash the ice cream off your body.

CONS Food in the bathroom is gross.

341. Under the Table at a Comedy Club

You can steal a dark corner and go at it like madmen, or you can slowly please each other from underneath the table under the premises of dropping something and bending down to get it.

BEST POSITION Game's On or Manual Stimulation

PROS It's unlikely you'll get caught, but make sure your knees don't show telltale signs of resting on them for long periods of time!

CONS Comedy clubs really pack in the people and the tables, so getting under the table may not be a real option, but you can figure something out.

342. At an Old-Fashioned Roller-Skating Rink

Why not go on a date to the roller-skating rink and sneak into the bathroom to have sex with your roller skates on?

BEST POSITION Standing Doggy Style or Bodyguard

PROS If they have a handicap bathroom stall (more roomy) Standing Doggy Style is great fun because you'll be rolling back and forth.

CONS It's hard enough to just stand up on skates. Try not to fall.

343. At an Olympic Complex

If you think having sex at your gym is exhilarating, try having sex with your partner at an Olympic complex! Try for an Olympic size orgasm!

BEST POSITION Anything goes!

PROS The whole idea of the Olympics is pushing yourself and achieving things that no one else can. Now apply this to your sex life.

CONS Be careful not to injure yourself in the attempt to "go for the gold."

344. On a Pier with the Waves Crashing Below

The sound of the ocean invokes nature's rhythm within our bodies. Head out on a pier for some evening sex among the waves.

BEST POSITION Standing Doggy Style or Bodyguard

PROS If you're careful, no one will even notice.

CONS Watch out for nosy fishermen and the things they leave behind like hooks and fish parts.

345. Behind a Large Display at a Wax Museum

Wax museums are fun to look at and all, but you can take this excursion to a whole new level by pretending to be a wax display doing the nasty.

BEST POSITION Dancer or Bodyguard

PROS What a fun way to turn a mundane wax museum tour into something raunchy and exciting!

CONS Don't want to get caught? Better hurry!

346. Behind the Stuffed Grizzly Bear at a Sports Store

Many sports stores have huge, stuffed grizzly bears that are on display. They're quite majestic, but even better when viewed from behind! Sneak behind the bear, lean up against the backside and get busy!

BEST POSITION Dancer or Bodyguard

PROS Never again does a woman have to be bored when her partner takes her to the sports store!

CONS Just don't tip over the grizzly!

347. On a River Boat Casino

Go gambling on a riverboat casino and take a chance on each other. Find a dark corner or empty hallway to grab a quickie.

BEST POSITION Dancer or Standing Doggy Style

PROS There's nothing like a game of chance to get your adrenalin and hormones flowing.

CONS Cameras are watching the entire casino floor, so you may end up the main feature for the casino guards who will be watching.

CHAPTER 9

BEST PLACES TO GET ARRESTED

Public sex is one thing, and yes, it comes with some risk of getting caught, fined, or arrested, but if you're really looking to push the envelope of getting thrown in jail, then here are some places you'll want to explore.

348. In a Public Official's Office

Have sex in your favorite Senator's office, if you can get an appointment, that is.

BEST POSITION Standing Doggy Style or Butterfly

PROS It's a very interesting way to stick it to the man.

CONS Getting in can be a challenge and you will likely be escorted off the premises.

349. On the Steps of the County Courthouse

Having sex on the courthouse steps just has a certain ring to it. It'll be easier to pull this one off if the courthouse has bushes or columns that you can hide behind.

BEST POSITION Games on or Delight

PROS The steps give you a place to sit.

CONS The are lots of law enforcement types hanging around.

350. In an Unused Room of the County Courthouse

Next time you're at the courthouse, sneak into a broom closet or supply room, block the door, and let it all hang out.

BEST POSITION Butterfly or Game's On.

PROS These rooms are rarely used, and it's very possible that you'll be undisturbed.

CONS It is a public building, so if you get caught, there could be consequences that may find you back in a courthouse for another reason.

351. In the Parking Lot of Your Local Police Precinct

This is a great way to add some adventure and risk to simply having sex in your car. Believe it or not, daytime is better for this one because you'll be less suspicious. You've heard the phrase "hiding in plain sight," right?

BEST POSITION Cowgirl or Deep Stick

PROS You're in your car, so if you do get caught you can blabber some excuse about losing an earring or pen under the seat.

CONS The jail cell is just inside.

352. In the Parking Lot of Any Other Local Government Building

Government buildings are surrounded by security cameras and guards these days, so while it's very likely that you'll get caught, it can still be fun to try.

BEST POSITION Game's On or Mastery

PROS Quickies in the car are awesome.

CONS There are tons of cameras and security guards.

353. On a Piece of City Construction Equipment

Just imagine having sex in the back of one of those giant dump trucks or a huge bulldozer! Bigger really is better in this case.

BEST POSITION Depends on the equipment. Be creative.

PROS Take a camera and get some pictures. It'll make for some great memories.

CONS The city doesn't like to share their toys. Don't get caught.

354. Next to the Washington Monument

Come on, who hasn't thought about it? There's nothing more phallic than the Washington Monument.

BEST POSITION Dancer or Standing Oral

PROS You'll have memories to last a lifetime.

CONS It's a very public place, so you'll have to be quick.

355. Some State Where Oral Sex Is Illegal

According to an article by San Francisco State University (*www .journalism.sfsu.edu*), oral sex is illegal in Alabama, Arizona, Florida, Idaho, Kansas, Louisiana, Massachusetts, Minnesota, Mississippi, Georgia, North and South Carolina, Oklahoma, Oregon, Rhode Island, Utah, Virginia, and Washington, D.C. So take your pick!

BEST POSITION Game's On and Spread Eagle, obviously

PROS You are standing up for your rights! Yes, the pun is intended!

CONS It's illegal, so you may get arrested if caught.

356. Anal Sex in a State Where Anal Sex Is Illegal

And here we go again—according to the same article from San Francisco State University (*www.journalism.sfsu.edu*), in Georgia those charged and convicted for either oral or anal sex can be sentenced to no less than one year and no more than twenty years imprisonment. So, have anal sex in Georgia and stand up for your rights.

BEST POSITION Rear Entry or Standing Doggy Style

PROS You are "bending over" for you rights!

CONS You have to ask—is it really worth the risk?

357. At the Mayor's House with the Mayor's Wife

Wanna get arrested? Then this is the way to go!

BEST POSITION Whichever position she likes the most.

PROS It will be an adventure!

CONS You may get arrested and/or shot. Technically, a police officer can arrest you for *what seems like* pretty much any reason, take you to jail, and then you have to hire a lawyer to be released. While that may not seem legal, it happens all the time. Some of the most common cases of this are for women going topless in public. So that's why we say be careful!

358. In a Public School Bus

Now this just seems like a bad idea—but this is the list of places to get you arrested. Don't do it when kids are around!

BEST POSITION Mastery or Lotus

PROS There are plenty of different options for positions on a school bus.

CONS Not only will you get arrested, you'll possibly even be listed as a sex offender for simply thinking about having sex where children sit.

359. In the Back of a Police Mobile Unit

If you have the right connections and can get access to a police mobile unit, yes, you guessed it, it's time for some more role play. Take turns arresting each other. Don't forget the handcuffs!

BEST POSITION Game's On or Lap Dance

PROS Role play doesn't get better than this.

CONS If you're on the police force, you could lose your job. If not, you could get arrested.

360. In a Jail Cell

Well, you've already been arrested; why not make the best of it (assuming that you're in the same cell)?

BEST POSITION Missionary or Bodyguard

PROS You'll have a great story to tell your grandchildren. *"I remember when your grandmother and I . . . "* And all the grandkids will groan.

CONS You could be sentenced to mandatory counseling for sex addiction, especially if you were arrested for doing it at one of the other places in this chapter.

361. Against the Glass in an Interrogation Room

Really wanna push your luck? Plaster yourselves up against the glass in the interrogation room.

BEST POSITION Bodyguard or Dancer

PROS The guys on the other side will enjoy the show.

CONS And then they'll take you back to your cell.

362. At a Swinger Club That Sells Alcohol

Now this is a little-known fact that we thought we'd share. The reason that on-premise (you can have sex there) swinger clubs are BYOB (Bring Your Own Bottle/Booze) is because there are some weird laws around being able to have sex at an establishment that sells alcohol. So if you've always wanted to get caught in the middle of a raid, frequent a swinger club that sells booze and allows people to have sex on the premises.

BEST POSITION Anything goes!

PROS It'll be great fun and you can see your picture on the evening news.

CONS Going to jail is not as fun as it first may seem.

CHAPTER 10

TRULY DANGEROUS SEX

Some of us love a good adrenaline rush. We thrive on fear and danger when others run and hide. Just as the title implies, all of the places in the section are associated with real danger—you can be injured or even killed trying to attempt have sex in these places.

363. In a Car Parked on the Railroad Tracks

This may seem like a good idea at first, but there are just too many things that could go wrong.

BEST POSITION Mastery or Deck Chair

PROS Dangerous sex can be very exciting.

CONS Uhhh . . . The potential for death, injury, and damage to your car is pretty high.

364. During Combat Training on an Artillery Field

And the rocket's red glare, the bombs bursting in air . . . It works for *The Star-Spangled Banner*, but maybe not for a sexual tryst.

BEST POSITION Missionary or Cowgirl

PROS It's like a giant fireworks show, only louder and more damaging to your eardrums.

CONS Is the thrill really worth the risk not only of personal injury but of being arrested by the military?

365. While Being Strangled or Held Underwater

Breath play is very popular and also very dangerous. Don't do it!

BEST POSITION Missionary or Doggy Style

PROS Many people claim to have stronger orgasms as they are about to pass out.

CONS The risk of death is way too high here. Just think about the various news stories you've heard about David Carradine (2009) and Michael Hutchence (1997). While the official cause of death is listed as asphyxiation, both are suspected to have died while practicing autoerotic asphyxiation.

366. On Top of a Moving Train

All the spies run around on top of the train in the movies—you can too!

BEST POSITION Missionary or Rear Entry

PROS The adrenaline rush of being on top of a moving train is incredible.

CONS You may fall off and die!

367. On Top of a Moving Bus

This one's not as glamorous, and it seems easy to fall off because buses make ninety-degree turns onto the next street, but they do move more slowly.

BEST POSITION Missionary or Rear Entry

PROS The adrenaline rush of being on top of a moving bus is incredible.

CONS You may fall off and die!

368. On the Side of a Telephone Poll

Put on your spike boots and cling together on the side of telephone poll.

BEST POSITION Bodyguard or Standing Missionary

PROS It's a totally unique and different experience.

CONS Don't fall off or get electrocuted!

369. High Up in a Tree

Remember what it's like to climb a tree? Climb up and have sex in the tree.

BEST POSITION Bodyguard or Mastery

PROS You'll truly feel like a wild animal.

CONS Don't fall off!

370. On a Really Tall Radio Tower

Water towers are just as good!

BEST POSITION Missionary or Deck Chair

PROS The view from up there is incredible.

CONS Don't fall off!

371. In the Back of a Pickup Truck While Driving Down the Freeway

While this may seem like a good idea and you see people riding in the back of pickup trucks all the time, there are no seat belts. Having said that, lying in the back of a pickup naked with the wind swirling around you sounds very sexy!

BEST POSITION Missionary or Spoons

PROS It's like being on a roller-coaster bed.

CONS The risk of injury and death if you're in an accident are too great.

372. In the Back of a Semi Truck While Driving Down the Freeway

This one seems a little less risky than the pickup but still feels romantic in a spy adventure sort of way.

BEST POSITION Dancer or Missionary

PROS Having sex while in a moving vehicle is exciting.

CONS You won't have the wind swirling around you, but you'll also not fly into oncoming traffic if there's an accident. You'll simply bounce around inside the truck!

373. On Top of the High Diving Board at an Olympic Pool

If you liked having sex on your own diving board, why not take it to the next level and have sex on a high dive!

BEST POSITION Missionary or Cowgirl

PROS You'll have an incredible view of the swim complex and you can jump in to cool off when you're finished.

CONS Diving boards are very narrow. Don't lose track of where you are or you could fall off.

374. In a Window-Washing Basket

Just imagine having sex while suspended eighty stories above the city streets! What a rush.

BEST POSITION Standing Oral or Bodyguard

PROS The added adrenalin can really enhance your sexual experience.

CONS There's always the possibility of falling out. Make sure to use the safety harnesses and don't get too crazy.

375. In a Bucket Truck with the Bucket as High as It Will Go

Create some electricity of your own while pretending to repair some phone or electric lines.

BEST POSITION Standing Doggy Style or Standing Oral

PROS You'll be in the air so you won't be noticed.

CONS There is a real danger of falling or getting fired if you work for the company who owns the bucket truck.

376. While Standing on a Secured Ladder

Role play. "Oh, please Mister Fireman, please save me from this burning building!" Seriously, you can do this one at home if you have a ladder.

BEST POSITION Modified Bodyguard—you need to hold on to the ladder

PROS Very erotic to be snuggled tightly on a ladder and knowing that you could fall at any minute.

CONS Unless the ladder is firmly secured to the building, there is a very real danger of falling.

377. While Hanging from a Trapeze

While not everyone is a trapeze artist, if you're interested, you can learn. It's exhilarating and fun, and learning the trapeze can give you flexibility that you can use in the bedroom too.

BEST POSITION Modified Cradle with him sitting on the trapeze bar or Modified Deep Stick with her hanging by her knees from the trapeze bar. This is a tricky maneuver and not for the uncoordinated!

PROS Hanging from a swing twenty feet in the air is exciting by itself. (We suggest no more than two feet in the air, or better yet in a sex swing that's made for this.)

CONS Once again, there is a real danger of falling. Make sure there's a net under you.

378. While Bungee Jumping

Strap yourselves together in a sexual position like standing Missionary or 69 and jump! If you're not ready for that, try bungee jumping naked.

BEST POSITION Missionary or 69

PROS What a rush!

CONS It's unlikely that you'll actually be able to have sex, but simply being in a sexual position while bungee jumping can still be quite invigorating.

379. While Hang Gliding Tandem Style

Strap in for a tandem (two-person) hang-gliding adventure that you'll never forget.

BEST POSITION Missionary or Rear Entry

PROS Having sex while flying like a bird can feel very freeing. Even simply hang gliding naked can be very freeing (and a little cold).

CONS Hang gliding attire does not lend itself to getting naked, so you'll have to get creative.

380. While Skydiving

Strap yourselves together for a freefall adventure. Save the sexual activity until the parachute is open and you're drifting down. You won't have long, but what a ride!

BEST POSITION Missionary or 69

PROS Having sex while floating through the sky is invigorating.

CONS You're limited to what you can actually do, and let's not forget the real danger of skydiving.

381. While Rappelling Down a Cliff over Scenic Views

Enjoy the view that only rappelling will give you with your partner in a new and totally different way. Use your imagination, as long as you don't remove any safety equipment to get into a sexual position.

BEST POSITION Bodyguard or Drill

PROS The privacy and the views are incredible.

CONS You could get tangled in the ropes and fall.

382. While Rock Climbing

Make an exhilarating rock climb even more fun by experiencing something new with your partner.

BEST POSITION Lotus or Deck Chair

PROS The views and the exhilaration of reaching the top create a euphoric feeling.

CONS There is a real danger of falling. Unlike rappelling, you're not hanging on to a rope.

383. On the Ledge of a High-Rise Building

Love heights? Then head up to the top floor of a high-rise and have sex on the ledge. Just make sure that the ledge is wide enough and ideally is enclosed behind a fence of some sort.

BEST POSITION Missionary or Lotus

PROS The view of course.

CONS Real danger of falling and pedestrians below may think you're attempting suicide.

384. In Your Car in the Summertime with the Windows Up

This one is under dangerous sex because of the very real danger of overheating. While getting all hot and sweaty together is quite erotic, there are less dangerous ways to do it—like the hot yoga room.

BEST POSITION Mastery or Deck Chair

PROS Who doesn't enjoy hot sweaty sex?

CONS There's a real danger of heatstroke or heat exhaustion.

CHAPTER 11

BEST PLACES TO HAVE SEX IN YOUR CAR

You car is your best friend when you're looking for new and interesting places for a sexual tryst. Some of the places in this list will look very familiar to you.

385. In an Alley in Your Neighborhood

When you get home from a date, stop in the alley for a quick romp in the car. It'll be worth the few extra minutes that you have to pay the babysitter.

BEST POSITION Game's On or Mastery

PROS You'll feel like a teenager again.

CONS Nosy neighbors may give you a hard time.

386. While Waiting in Line at the Bank Drive-Up Window

Waiting in line at the bank doesn't have to be boring anymore.

BEST POSITION Game's On or Mastery

PROS You're in your car, so you may get some weird looks, but that's about it.

CONS Don't forget that the speaker to the tellers is always on. You may end up giving the entire audience inside the bank a good show.

387. While Waiting in Line at a Fast-Food Drive Through

Waiting in line for junk food doesn't have to be boring anymore either!

BEST POSITION Game's On or Mastery

PROS You'll be able to immediate satisfy your post-sex munchies.

CONS Don't try this at McDonald's. They've really got it together. You barely have time to get the money ready before they hand over the food!

388. Parked Down the Street from Junior's Soccer Practice

Not *at* junior's soccer practice, but down the street from practice—well down the street.

BEST POSITION Deck Chair or Mastery

PROS It's a fun way to wait for soccer practice to end.

CONS Junior may ask why you're suddenly both coming to soccer practice.

389. Next to a Traffic Meter

Put your quarters in and go! Park on a city street next to a meter—it's cheaper than a hotel for a lunchtime rendezvous. This one works best if you have dark tinted windows.

BEST POSITION Deck Chair or Mastery

PROS It's a great place for a quickie if you just can't wait!

CONS Watch out for the meter attendants, or you may be paying for more than a parking ticket.

390. In a Hotel Parking Garage

When looking for a place to have sex in your car, never underestimate parking garages. Hotel parking garages are great because they're not very busy.

BEST POSITION Deck Chair or Mastery

PROS They're typically dark and quiet.

CONS Many hotels charge very high rates if you're not a guest.

391. In a Downtown Office Building Parking Garage

For a slightly lower fee, you can park in a downtown parking garage. It's still a great option for a last-minute quickie.

BEST POSITION Deck Chair or Mastery

PROS It's slightly less expensive than a hotel parking garage.

CONS For some reason these parking garages tend to be more open and busy.

392. In a Bentley GT Continental

Okay, since we're talking about sex in cars, there are a few cars that you just have to try. The Bentley is one of them. It's so plush inside that it's like having sex on a small cloud.

BEST POSITION Mastery or Lap Dance

PROS It's so plush!

CONS It's too small to lie down in the back seat.

393. In a Maserati Quattroporte

For those of you who don't know, Maserati doesn't only make tiny little high-speed sports cars. They also make a really plush sedan that just happens to go from 0 to 60 miles per hour in less than six seconds!

BEST POSITION Deck Chair or Mastery

PROS It's so plush!

CONS It attracts a lot of attention!

394. In a Dodge Viper

It just looks cool, so why not?

BEST POSITION Mastery or Lap Dance

PROS It looks really cool.

CONS The interior is uncomfortable so you may be better off leaning on the hood.

395. In a Hummer

Okay, a Hummer isn't a car, but you have to check this one off your list. If you don't have access to a Hummer, go take one for a test drive. Sure you could do the same in an Escalade, but it doesn't sound as good as "Humping in the Hummer."

BEST POSITION Drill or Spread Eagle

PROS It's much roomier than a car.

CONS Low head room—be careful not to bump your head.

396. At a Drive-In Movie

This may have been more popular in our parents' generation, but if you can still find a drive-in movie, it's great fun!

BEST POSITION Game's On or Mastery

PROS Everyone expects you to make out in your car at a drive-in movie.

CONS You may miss the movie.

397. In the Car at a Drive-In Restaurant

Go to a drive-in restaurant like Sonic and hop in the back seat to fool around while you're waiting for your food or as a quickie for dessert.

BEST POSITION Game's On or Lap Dance

PROS It will make you feel young again.

CONS Try not to get ketchup in your hair.

398. Along the San Juan Skyway

Driving around the San Juan Skyway in Colorado is one of the most scenic ways to view the amazing surroundings of the state. Pull over at one of the many scenic outlooks.

BEST POSITION Cowgirl or Deck Chair

PROS Don't forget to check out the incredible views.

CONS Watch out for State Troopers.

399. At a Rest Area on the Side of the Freeway

Next time you're on a long road trip, pull over at a rest area to break the monotony of the long drive. Just be aware of a few things: Some rest areas are very busy, and others are very desolate and could be dangerous.

BEST POSITION Standing Doggy Style or Butterfly on the hood of the car

PROS It definitely makes the drive more enjoyable.

CONS Beware of your surroundings.

400. Driving in Your Car During Heavy Traffic

While sex in a moving car is not recommended, especially if you're the driver, if you're only going five miles an hour it can be a little safer.

BEST POSITION Game's On or Manual Stimulation

PROS It's a great way to avoid road rage.

CONS Don't mistake the accelerator for the brake pedal in the heat of the moment.

401. On the Side of the Road During Heavy Traffic

This is by far the safer option. If traffic isn't moving anyway, why not pull over to the side for a quickie? You can even try this one by yourself if you're stuck in traffic alone.

BEST POSITION Game's On or Manual Stimulation

PROS You're far less likely to get into an accident this way.

CONS If you don't have tinted windows, rubberneckers may cause an accident.

402. On the Side of the Road on Your Motorcycle

Okay, so it's not a car, but motorcycles offer some great flexibility for positions without the limited headroom.

BEST POSITION Mastery or Spread Eagle

PROS No ceiling to bump your head.

CONS No privacy, so you'll need a secluded place to pull over.

403. Inside an Antique Car at a Flea Market

Antique cars are often tucked away in the back rooms of flea markets, providing the perfect private place for a morning sex session!

BEST POSITION Cowgirl or Deck Chair

PROS Enjoy the nostalgia of getting in the back seat of a '57 Chevy or something similar.

CONS It's in the back room of a flea market so it's most likely not been detailed (or cleaned) in a while.

404. On a Ferry Boat

Turn an ordinary ferry ride into a titillating encounter between you and your partner.

BEST POSITION Cowgirl or Deck Chair

PROS This is yet another place to have sex in your car.

CONS It's pretty public, so if you're adverse to getting caught, try to find the least visited area of the ferry you can or wait until it gets dark.

405. In the Mall Parking Garage

Take a break from shopping or enjoy a quickie before going inside. It may seem a little juvenile, but who cares!

BEST POSITION Cowgirl or Deck Chair

PROS Most parking garages at the mall are pretty dark, so it shouldn't be too challenging to find a dark corner.

CONS Mall security can get a little annoying.

406. In the Trunk of a Cadillac (Lid Open!)

Have one of those big Cadillacs with the huge trunks? A pink one? Even better! Grab a blanket and a few pillows and climb in.

BEST POSITION 69 or Deck Chair

PROS It's truly unique.

CONS It may be challenging to find a good position, especially if you're very tall.

407. In Your Car While Going Through an Automated Car Wash

While you won't have time for intercourse, it's a great place for oral or a hand job.

BEST POSITION Game's On or Manual Stimulation

PROS It's fun to be pulled along through the water and bubbles.

CONS Set your watch because you have about three minutes.

408. Near a Railroad or Subway Track

Find a place to park as close to the railroad track as possible, but still a safe distance from the passing train. Roll the windows down so that you can get the full affect of the sound and wind from the trains passing by.

BEST POSITION Cowgirl or Deck Chair

PROS It's a great way to add a sense of adventure to your lovemaking.

CONS Most railway tracks are not in the best parts of town, so stay aware of your surroundings.

409. While Driving Across the Golden Gate Bridge

The Golden Gate Bridge is one of the most beautiful bridges in the world. The bridge is 1.7 miles long and can get very busy. Keep in mind that it is a toll bridge, so bring your dollars.

BEST POSITION Game's On or Manual Stimulation

PROS This is another great way to see one of the United States's great tourist attractions.

CONS One of you may miss the scenery.

410. While Driving Across the Seven Mile Bridge in Florida

The Seven Mile Bridge, in the Florida Keys, runs over a channel between the Gulf of Mexico and the Florida Strait.

BEST POSITION Game's On or Manual Stimulation

PROS This is another must-see attraction.

CONS As with some of the others, one of you will likely miss the scenery.

CHAPTER 12

BEST PLACES TO HAVE SEX "ON THE MOVE"

All of the places in this section have one thing in common—they are on or in moving locations.

411. On an Amusement Park Ride of Your Choice

Add some spice to the tunnel of love or the log ride by getting freaky.

BEST POSITION Mastery or Cowgirl

PROS You'll be surprised at your new-found creativity.

CONS Watch out for the kiddos and maybe stick to the less busy rides.

412. On the Rotor-Ride at the Carnival

You know, it's the one where you stand up against the wall and the room spins? Once the room is spinning fast enough, the floor drops out.

BEST POSITION Missionary or Bodyguard

PROS What a cool way to have sex!

CONS Will it really work with one on top of the other? Maybe stick to a side position.

413. On the Parachute Ride at Six Flags

Get into one of the baskets rather than the benches, and get in some sexy action on the way up and on the way down.

BEST POSITION Standing Doggy Style or Standing Oral

PROS This one's very easy to implement.

CONS It's doubtful you'll have time to have actual intercourse.

414. While Going Down a Long Water Slide

Whether on a tube or tangled together, enjoy sexy fun on the way down.

BEST POSITION Missionary or Mastery

PROS It's wet and slippery fun.

CONS This is another one where you may or may not be able to have intercourse, but it'll sure be fun trying.

415. In a Canoe Floating Down the River

A ride in a canoe can be fun and relaxing, but a romp in a canoe can be even more fun! Remember, canoes can tip very easily. Also make sure that you're floating down a lazy river rather than on fast moving water.

BEST POSITION Mastery or Cowgirl

PROS The scenery and being one with nature are amazing.

CONS Canoe trips are normally with large groups of people so privacy may be limited. Even lazy rivers move—who's driving the boat?

416. In a Convertible Driving with the Top Down

As with all sex in the car, ideally someone else is driving. If not, just be very careful and keep both hands on the wheel. You can also pull over to the side of the road for a safer romp in the sun.

BEST POSITION Mastery or Cowgirl

PROS The sun and wind in your hair invokes a feeling of adventure.

CONS Sunburn and windburn—bring your sunscreen.

417. In a Dune Buggy Riding Through the Desert

Turn an ordinary dune buggy excursion into a fun and exciting one by going off the beaten path and finding somewhere you can get down and dirty in your buggy.

BEST POSITION Standing Doggy Style over the windshield or Cowgirl

PROS If you have sex while driving, at least it's a little safer than driving down the freeway.

CONS Dust can get everywhere. Really, everywhere.

418. In a Golf Cart

What better way to knock a hole in one than on a late-night encounter on the golf course? Have your lady sit on your lap for a ride down the golf course. The bumping of the golf cart is sure to get you going!

BEST POSITION Lap Dance or Cowgirl

PROS It's probably one of the safer "sex while driving" options.

CONS There's a small chance that you'll lose your golf membership.

419. While Riding the Gondola at Sea World

See the sites and have adult fun at the same time. Unlike some of the bigger ski lifts, the gondolas at Sea World are small enough that you can have one to yourselves.

BEST POSITION Lap Dance or Mastery

PROS You'll be up above the crowd.

CONS The gondolas are open air, so try not to fall out.

420. While Riding the Skyfari Aerial Tram at the San Diego Zoo

Riding over the San Diego Zoo provides beautiful views of the zoo and surrounding parks.

BEST POSITION Lap Dance or Mastery

PROS You'll be up above the crowd.

CONS The trams are open air, so be careful not to fall out.

421. While Riding in a Hot Air Balloon

This is actually a very common sexual fantasy/goal. It seems that everyone wants to have sex in a hot air balloon. Good for you! Just keep something in mind, unless you're a balloon pilot, there will be a third person in the balloon with you.

BEST POSITION Bodyguard or Standing Oral

PROS Wow—the views and the silence.

CONS Space is limited and you have to be aware of possible turbulence.

422. In a Private Jet

If you're going to join the mile-high club, why not do it in style? You can try to cram yourself into a public lavatory, or sneak a feel in the seat, or you can enjoy mile-high sex in every position imaginable on a private jet.

BEST POSITION Anything goes!

PROS Luxury and privacy.

CONS Cost. Chartering a private jet starts at around $1,500 per hour.

423. In a Prop Plane

While not as luxurious as a private jet, it's still better than having sex while flying commercial. The size of the plane will determine what you can really do, but at least it'll be better than the lavatory on a commercial airline.

BEST POSITION Lap Dance or Game's On

PROS It's more affordable than chartering a private jet.

CONS It's not going to be as comfortable as a private jet.

424. While Taking a Helicopter Tour

This is an interesting twist on the "not-so-mile-high" club. Helicopters come in all shapes and sizes and once again, remember that unless you're the pilot, there'll be someone else there.

BEST POSITION Lap Dance or Game's On

PROS See the sites and have sex while flying.

CONS It's still not as nice as the private jet.

425. In a Jeep While Driving Through Rugged Terrain

If you've ever had the opportunity to drive a Jeep through rugged terrain, you know how much fun it is. Combine that with a sexual experience and you've taken it to a whole new level!

BEST POSITION Mastery or Lap Dance

PROS It feels rugged and primal.

CONS Really rough terrain will make it very challenging to maintain any position!

426. In a Jeep While Driving Through Wet Mud

Take it to the next level in the Jeep by driving through wet mud or water. This is something right out of a steamy romance novel. She's being whisked away by the adventurous mountain stud.

BEST POSITION Mastery or Lap Dance

PROS It feels even more rugged and primal.

CONS Mud everywhere! Your car might get stuck.

427. In a Ride-Through Cave

Boy it sure is dark isn't it? In a ride-thru cave, you're in a Jeep with other people most of the time. Grab the back row and stick to manual or oral stimulation until you get outside again.

BEST POSITION Game's On or Manual Stimulation

PROS It's a good way to turn a slightly interesting tour into a very interesting one.

CONS Where do you find a ride-through cave other than Branson, Missouri?

428. In a Commercial Airplane Lavatory

This is what most people think of when they think of joining the mile-high club. While it's not the first choice for sex in the sky, it's one of those places that you just have experience so that you can check it off your list.

BEST POSITION Bodyguard or Standing Doggy Style

PROS You can lock the door.

CONS It's a very small space that typically doesn't smell very good.

429. In the Back of a Taxi

While not very original, why not take advantage of having a driver and enjoy some back seat sexual adventures on the way to the airport?

BEST POSITION Game's On or Mastery

PROS Someone else is driving.

CONS The taxi driver may not approve of what you're doing, or he may have an accident because he's so distracted watching you.

430. In the Back Seat of a Limousine

This is even better than the back seat of a taxi. Hire a limo for a few hours and just tell the driver to drive you around town. Have him close the privacy screen and enjoy!

BEST POSITION Mastery or Drill

PROS You have room and privacy to explore your fantasies.

CONS It can be a little pricey but well worth it.

431. In the Back Seat of a Greyhound Bus

Riding in the back of the bus is a favorite spot for teenagers who want to make out. Why not feel like a teenager again and do it too?

BEST POSITION Mastery or Lap Dance

PROS If you take a nighttime bus ride, it'll be dark and most people will be sleeping.

CONS The back seat of a Greyhound bus can be both loud and filled with the smell of diesel fumes.

432. On a Bareback Horse

Ride 'em cowboy. Explore the California coast on a beach horse ride! Having sex on a bareback horse is something straight out of a steamy romance novel.

BEST POSITION Mastery or Lap Dance

PROS A very high romance level.

CONS Implementation can be challenging—it's easy to fall off the horse.

433. On a Camel's Back

Do something a little different and go for a camel ride, only make the camel ride much more fun than it is at first glance.

BEST POSITION Mastery or Lap Dance

PROS It's truly unique.

CONS Camels spit and bite!

434. On a Catamaran in the Middle of the Lake

Enjoy sailing even more by getting naked on a Catamaran in the middle of the lake. These days Catamarans come in all shapes and sizes, but the idea here is the smaller sail boats with a flat deck between two pontoons.

BEST POSITION Missionary or 69

PROS You can go wherever you want and get totally naked.

CONS Bring sunscreen so that you don't get a sunburn.

435. On a Fast, Thrilling Roller Coaster

Go for a thrill ride on a roller coaster with your partner. Enjoy all the thrill of the coaster and the pleasure of sexual stimulation at the same time!

BEST POSITION This one's limited to Manual Stimulation

PROS It's an incredible adrenaline rush.

CONS It might not be possible to get very far sexually, but trying is what counts!

436. Under a Trench Coat on the Bus

Feeling adventurous? Wearing nothing but your trench coat, take a bus ride and let your partner pleasure you under your coat.

BEST POSITION Manual Stimulation or Lap Dance

PROS Enjoy the excitement of being naked under your coat.

CONS You may not actually be able to have intercourse on a busy bus ride.

437. In an Inner Tube on a Lazy River Ride

Relax and enjoy the ride—with your partner that is! Snuggle up together in a single tube and get sensual, but you'd be better off sticking with a single position.

BEST POSITION Lotus or Mastery

PROS It's relaxing, sensual, and romantic.

CONS Changing positions without tipping over is nearly impossible.

438. While Riding on a Jet Ski

A jet ski is basically just a motorcycle on the water. Go out to the middle of the lake and have a go with each other.

BEST POSITION Mastery or Lap Dance

PROS The motion of the jet ski moving across the water can provide incredible sensations.

CONS Your life vests can get in the way.

439. White Water Rapids Ride

The water is typically very cold and the adrenalin levels are much higher.

BEST POSITION Mastery or Lap Dance

PROS This is an incredible rush.

CONS You'll likely be in a boat with other people so pick the right crew!

440. At the Park on a Merry-Go-Round

There are an exciting number of positions available on a merry-go-round when you use the bars for support.

BEST POSITION Standing Doggy Style or Missionary

PROS The motion of the merry-go-round can add an exciting element to sex.

CONS You might get a little dizzy!

441. Riverboat Cruise

A dinner cruise takes you away from the mundane life for a few hours.

BEST POSITION Standing Doggy Style or Dancer

PROS Riverboat cruises can be beautiful and romantic.

CONS Don't get too crazy on the boat railing. You wouldn't want to end up in the water.

442. On an Old-Fashioned Steamboat Ride

Spend a Saturday afternoon taking a steamboat ride. It's a fun and new way to get intimate with your partner, and to stave off boredom.

BEST POSITION Standing Doggy Style or Dancer

PROS Steamboats remind us of a slower, more relaxed era.

CONS Avoid the boiler room. It'll be hot and dirty.

443. On A Ski Lift

Enjoy the ride up the mountain with some sexual fun. You'll probably be limited to Manual Stimulation or oral, but you'll be warmer when you get to the top.

BEST POSITION Manual Stimulation or Game's On

PROS It's a great way to enjoy the ride up the mountain.

CONS The goal of ski attire is to cover every inch of your skin and to keep the cold out—making it challenging for a quickie.

444. While Riding in a Speedboat

Many speedboats travel in excess of 70 miles per hour across the water. You'll need someone else to drive but don't be shy, maybe you can repay the favor and drive while the other couple enjoys themselves.

BEST POSITION Standing Doggy Style or Lap Dance

PROS It's an incredibly thrilling ride.

CONS Rough water can make sexual activity more challenging.

445. While Riding in a Pontoon Boat

A pontoon boat is a completely different feel. You can enjoy the gentle rocking and a much slower pace with your lovemaking.

BEST POSITION Missionary or Mastery

PROS You can putt across the lake at a very relaxing and romantic speed.

CONS Someone has to drive the boat.

446. On a Houseboat That You've Rented for the Weekend

A houseboat is like a hotel room on the water. You can anchor in the middle of the lake or close to shore. The possibilities are unlimited!

BEST POSITION Anything goes!

PROS It's on my list of top summer weekend getaways.

CONS Houseboats can be expensive, but you can cut costs by inviting a few of your open-minded and sexy friends.

447. While Being Pulled Behind a Boat in a Tube

Feeling adventurous? Let's get freaky "behind" the boat.

BEST POSITION Mastery or Rear Entry

PROS You're out in the middle of the lake, so anything goes!

CONS Staying on the tube can be challenging if the water is rough or if the driver goes too fast.

448. While Being Pulled Behind a Boat on a Hot Dog

A hot dog is one of those inflatable "hot dog" looking things that you see behind boats on the lake. It works best for sitting positions rather than lying down positions.

BEST POSITION Mastery or Lap Dance

PROS You're out in the middle of the lake, so anything goes! On that topic, you can have several people on the hot dog at the same time!

CONS Staying on the hot dog can be challenging if the water is rough or if the driver goes too fast.

449. On a Wakeboard

This is the most difficult of the "behind the boat" options. One person will be on the wakeboard with knees strapped in and the other will literally be riding in his or her lap!

BEST POSITION Mastery or Lap Dance—Hold on tight!

PROS It's a way to challenge yourself both physically and sexually.

CONS The person on bottom needs to be a great wakeboarder.

450. Riding in a Stagecoach

Take yourselves back to the Wild West by bouncing around naked in the back of a stagecoach. Many tourist spots offer stagecoach tours. The only trick is to book the coach for just the two of you.

BEST POSITION Lap Dance or Mastery

PROS Most stage coaches are fully enclosed, so you'll have plenty of privacy.

CONS Stage coaches are incredibly rough riding.

451. While Riding on a Scenic Open-Air Train

Enjoy the view and a little sexy fun on an old-fashioned open-air train. Many of these touristy rides offer dinner tours at dusk. It can be really romantic.

BEST POSITION Lap Dance or Manual Stimulation

PROS The beautiful scenery and nostalgia of being on an old-fashioned open-air train.

CONS By definition, it's very open, so privacy will be limited. You'll need to be very discreet in your actions.

452. On an Amtrak Train

Amtrak offers private sleeping quarters, so you can think of it as a hotel on wheels. Book a scenic trip across town or across the country and enjoy some private time away from the world.

BEST POSITION Anything goes!

PROS You'll have all the privacy you need.

CONS The living quarters a quite small.

453. On a High-Speed Train

Snuggle up with your lover while your train car passes beautiful scenery—at 100 miles per hour! According to Wikipedia, the Acela Express traveling from Boston to Washington, D.C., is the only high-speed train in operation in the United States and it really only averages 86 miles per hour but, hey, work with what you've got!

BEST POSITION Mastery or Lap Dance

PROS It's a safe way to have sex at 100 miles per hour.

CONS Airline type seating only—there are no private sleeping quarters.

454. While Driving in Your Car on a Secluded Highway

While this is safer than driving in traffic, it's still very dangerous because you're in a moving car. Having said that, there's something exhilarating about being naked and playing around in a moving car.

BEST POSITION Mastery or Game's On

PROS It's slightly safer than driving on the freeway.

CONS It's still very dangerous, unless you can get someone else to drive you.

455. While Parasailing

As if parasailing is not fun enough, you can add some sexual tension to the ride. Unless you have a custom harness, it's doubtful you can actually have intercourse, but a good first step is to parasail naked.

BEST POSITION Manual Simulation or Mastery (depending of the layout of the rigging)

PROS Having sex while floating like a bird can be so freeing.

CONS The harness and rigging make this difficult. You'll have to figure out how to strap yourselves in together—or use some trapeze moves.

456. On a Moving Motorcycle

This brings pictures of really bad boys and girls to mind. Take this opportunity to explore your bad side. Just don't forget your helmet.

BEST POSITION Mastery on a Harley or Missionary on a crotch rocket

PROS You get to wear leather.

CONS Very dangerous—make sure to practice standing still before attempting this while moving.

457. While Sledding in the Snow

Bring back childhood memories of sledding in the snow by going on a fun, sexy ride with your lover.

BEST POSITION Doggy Style or Mastery

PROS It's thrilling to feel a little out of control.

CONS You can run into a tree so wear proper safety gear.

458. Riding on a Snowmobile

Unlike a jet ski, this is a cold weather adventure. Take advantage of the fact that you can go places in the snow that most other vehicles can't get to.

BEST POSITION Standing Doggy Style or Mastery

PROS Normally accessible places become inaccessible in the snow, unless you have a snowmobile.

CONS It's definitely easy to get cold so don't strip all the way down if you don't want frostbite!

459. While Surfing in the Middle of the Ocean

Lie back on a surfboard in the middle of the ocean and go to town like the marine life under you does!

BEST POSITION Rear Entry or Mastery

PROS The sun is a natural aphrodisiac.

CONS Keeping your balance will be incredibly difficult. Practice in shallow water to get the hang of it.

460. While Windsurfing

Windsurfing is exhilarating, exciting, and a jolt to your senses. Feel the wind in your hair and on your face while feeling your partner on other parts of your body!

BEST POSITION Bodyguard or Standing Oral

PROS Once again, the sun is a natural aphrodisiac.

CONS You'll have be a very good windsurfer before even attempting this one.

461. In a Wind Tunnel

Have sex on the hood of an aerodynamic sports car in a wind tunnel. It'll give you feeling of driving down the road at 100 miles per hour.

BEST POSITION Missionary or Rear Entry

PROS The exhilaration of speed—perceived speed anyway.

CONS You'll have to stick to aerodynamic positions to avoid being blown off the car.

462. On a Ferris Wheel at Night

While the ferris wheel is loading and unloading, enjoy some sexual activities with your partner. According to an article from Gizmag (*www.gizmag.com/americas-largest-ferris-wheel/8859/*), the Pepsi Globe is the largest ferris wheel in America and when complete (perhaps in 2010) will offer sweeping vistas of the New York skyline.

BEST POSITION Mastery or Lap Dance

PROS You can enjoy the view in a new passionate way.

CONS The space will be tight, so you'll have to work around that.

CHAPTER 13

TRULY JUVENILE PLACES TO HAVE SEX

Bring back those feelings of first times, raging hormones, and sneaking around to make out. All of the places in this section will bring back the teenager in you! Many of these places are where kids actually hang out so please be very careful of your surroundings and always watch out for actual minors in the area.

463. At Church Camp

This is one of the biggest ironies of our time. How many young kids have lost their virginity at church camp? Think about it. They're away from parents with little supervision—it's the perfect opportunity!

BEST POSITION Missionary or Cowgirl

PROS There'll be plenty of opportunities to sneak away from the group, just like when you were younger.

CONS You're an adult—you can't do that! Just kidding.

464. At Band Camp

"One time at band camp . . . " Fill in your kinky freaky sex story here.

BEST POSITION Anything goes at band camp!

PROS You're the adult now so you'll have free reign to come and go as you please.

CONS Other adults and chaperones will not approve if you're caught.

465. At Chuck E. Cheese

Don't you think you've had to attend enough birthday parties for kids? Spend some grownup time playing your own "games."

BEST POSITION Dancer or Standing Oral

PROS You'll get to see who's really more competitive.

CONS There's a high kid density, so pay attention to who's watching you.

466. On a High School Classroom Desk

Why not act out your Mrs. Robinson fantasy? If you're too young to know who that is, then just have fun!

BEST POSITION Mastery or Lap Dance

PROS Come on, we've all thought about it one time or another.

CONS Depending on the shape of the desk, finding a comfortable position could be challenging.

467. On an Elementary School Classroom Desk

Remember those little desks (or tables and chairs) from elementary school. They're just the right height to have some fun. Besides, it just feels a little kinky!

BEST POSITION Mastery or Lap Dance

PROS The little chairs are at the right height for some fun new angles.

CONS The little chairs are made for little people and may not support your full weight.

468. On the Teacher's Desk

Can you think of a better way to get back at your teacher? Even better, try it with your teacher! You can even try a little teacher-student role play. The naughty schoolgirl is one of the most popular fantasies there is.

BEST POSITION Butterfly or Standing Doggy Style

PROS It's a great opportunity for some role play.

CONS If you're the teacher, you could lose your job.

469. In the Closet at a Friend's Party

Sneak into the closet for a little game of spin the bottle. It feels so juvenile and yet so fun.

BEST POSITION Dancer or Bodyguard

PROS You're an adult now, so if you get caught it'll be good for a laugh.

CONS It may be challenging to find a roomy closet that's not filled with all sorts of junk.

470. On the Bed in an Empty Bedroom at Your Friend's Party

When you were young, it was so hard to find a few minutes to just be alone with your sweetie. Bring that feeling back into your relationship.

BEST POSITION Deep Stick or Rear Entry—basically anything goes here!

PROS It can be very romantic.

CONS You may miss the party, but is that really so bad?

471. College Dorm Room

Having sex with a hot college chick is every man's fantasy. Make your partner's fantasies come true by sneaking off into your kid's dorm room for some hot sex while he or she is out with their friends.

BEST POSITION Missionary or Cowgirl

PROS Cheerleader outfit—duh!

CONS The word "a-w-k-ward!" comes to mind if your child catches you.

472. College Student Union

There's always furniture, including couches, tables, and chairs to lounge around on. Take advantage of it! Go in at night when it's about to close. There will be less of a crowd then.

BEST POSITION Delight or Standing Doggy Style

PROS Most college students couldn't care less if you're having sex on the sofa.

CONS Campus security might get you on tape, but it's not like they can suspend you (if you're not a student there!).

473. Frat House or Sorority House

Frat and sorority houses are notorious for their raunchy goings on. Get in on the fun by sneaking into one if you're not already a member and getting down and dirty.

BEST POSITION Standing Oral or Lap Dance

PROS If you're out of school, it's a great way to experience that old college nostalgia for a little while before you have to go back to your responsible life.

CONS Most fraternities are not fond of nonmembers being in their houses.

474. On a High School Track at Night

There's just something about the school track and football field at night that brings back memories of high school and gets those prepubescent hormones raging.

BEST POSITION Standing Oral or Dancer

PROS There should be plenty of shadows to conceal your activities.

CONS It may be challenging to get comfortable, but was that really the concern when you were in high school?

475. On the Top Bunk of Your Old Bunk Bed at Your Grandparent's House

There isn't anything more juvenile than having sex on the top bed of a bunk bed, especially the one that your Grandpa bought for you when you were a kid.

BEST POSITION Missionary or Cowgirl

PROS It just feels naughty.

CONS Make sure the bunk bed is very sturdy and well made, otherwise you may come crashing to the floor. It was made to hold the weight of a ten-year-old, and you're not ten anymore.

476. In the Hallway or Bathroom at Your Old High School

Write yourself a hall pass and sneak down a hallway for a quickie in the bathroom or deserted hallway. The best time to do this is when school is out of session and maybe at your five-, ten-, or twenty-five-year reunion!

BEST POSITION Dancer in the bathroom or Bodyguard against the lockers

PROS Remember hall passes? This is a chance for revenge.

CONS You made get surprised by a shocked janitor.

477. At a McDonald's Playplace

Revisit your childhood in an entirely new way. Make sure there aren't any children that will get an eyeful and don't leave anything behind. The best time is late in the evening after the children have gone home to bed.

BEST POSITION Doggy Style or Standing Oral

PROS It doesn't get more juvenile than this.

CONS There is a risk of being caught by children, so be careful. You could always, very easily, get arrested!

478. In the Back of an Ice Cream Truck

Bring back that childhood nostalgia by having sex in an ice cream truck. If there are any frozen treats in the back, use one to wet your mouth before oral sex, or lick melted ice cream off your partner's body for added sensations.

BEST POSITION 69 or Game's On

PROS Everyone loves ice cream!

CONS It can definitely get a little chilly so bring a blanket.

479. At the Local Lovers' Lane

Every town, big or small, has a well-known spot where people go to make out. Make it a point to find yours and go there.

BEST POSITION Cowgirl or Deck Chair

PROS This is another great place to have sex in your car.

CONS Unfortunately, most of these places are well known by local law enforcement.

480. At Your Parents' House While They're Home

Sneak into the bathroom, or even your bedroom while staying with your parents over the holidays. Let your parents wonder what you're up to but don't keep them waiting too long or they might come looking for you.

BEST POSITION Standing Doggy Style or Mastery in the bathroom

PROS It just feels so mischievous!

CONS If your parents are of like mind, they'll embarrass the heck out of you when you're done.

481. On a College Basketball Court at Night

If you're lucky enough to be affiliated with a college with a successful basketball team, this can be very nostalgic. Sneak in after everyone else is gone and have fun in the bleachers, on the court, under the goal posts, and even in the locker room.

BEST POSITION Dancer or Bodyguard

PROS The energy and excitement is very high after a winning basketball game.

CONS Watch out for campus security.

482. In the Recreation Center on the Pinball Machine

How long has it been since you've played a good game of pinball? It's very common to see people banging around and shaking the machine. It may go completely unnoticed if you put your partner between you and the pinball machine.

BEST POSITION Butterfly or Dancer

PROS It's a very juvenile and public place to have sex.

CONS If there are other people around, it's very likely that you'll be kicked out.

483. In Your Car Parked in Front of Your Parents' House

Recall those old high school days when you used to have to make out in the car. Why not bring back the memories with your current partner?

BEST POSITION Cowgirl or Deck Chair

PROS It's one of the best places for a quickie.

CONS You might get caught by your parents. Chances are they still won't approve.

484. On the Front Porch of Your Parents' House

Remember what it was like when you were a teenager and you had to steal a kiss on the front porch before sneaking into the house thirty minutes late? Next time you visit your parents, spend a few extra minutes making out on the front porch before you ring the door bell.

BEST POSITION Dancer or Bodyguard

PROS It just feels naughty, incredibly intimate, and romantic.

CONS Your parents may catch you.

485. In the Back Seat with Your Mom or Dad Driving

This one may be a little uncomfortable for many of you, but give it a try.

BEST POSITION Manual Stimulation or Lap Dance

PROS It'll keep you young—and horny!

CONS You may not feel comfortable having intercourse, but some heavy petting would be okay, wouldn't it?

486. In Your Lover's Childhood Room While His or Her Parents Are Home

Having sex in your partner's childhood bedroom just feels bad, but in such a good way. It's especially good if his or her parents have not remodeled his or her room since he or she was a child.

BEST POSITION Missionary or Standing Oral

PROS It's a kinky way to relive your childhood.

CONS Your partner's parents may strongly disapprove.

487. Under the Bleachers During a High School Football Game

Find a local high school whose football team is doing really well. This will ensure that the stadium is packed and that everyone's attention will be on the game. Sneak under the bleachers and find a dark shadow for a quickie.

BEST POSITION Dancer or Standing Oral

PROS It's very spontaneous.

CONS If you get caught, it's likely that you'll get kicked out and maybe arrested.

488. While Playing Laser Tag

And some adult fun to your next game of laser tag. When your partner tags you, they get an adult treat. Given that laser tag is also fun for kids; you'll need to do this late at night or just keep score for later.

BEST POSITION Standing Oral or Manual Stimulation

PROS It's a great new way to add excitement to a game of laser tag.

CONS Finding privacy can be challenging. This can be overcome by booking a private party for just you and your partner.

CHAPTER 14

BEST PLACES TO *REALLY* LET GO AND RELEASE INHIBITIONS

The biggest sexual issues that many of us face are self-created—yes, self-created. We are afraid to talk about sex, we are too shy to run around naked, we're afraid of what others might say or think. Well it's time to flush all of those limiting fears down the proverbial toilet. The places in this section encourage you to let loose and discover your inner sexual beast.

489. During a Session with a Professional Sex Therapist

You want a better sex life? Hire a professional to help you work through your issues as individuals and as a couple. Trust me. We all have our issues and they manifest in some of the weirdest ways.

BEST POSITION Anything goes!

PROS You'll have a better sex life because of the experience.

CONS Make sure that it's a qualified sex therapist and not just a pervert who likes to watch.

490. Handcuffed to the Bed in a Five-Star Hotel

Since you've shelled out your dollars for a five-star hotel, why not get kinky freaky. For some reason, we tend to let go when we're on vacation, so really let loose and release your inhibitions in this luxurious environment.

BEST POSITION Rear Entry or Deep Stick

PROS Cold hard steel and a luxurious bed. Ahhh.

CONS Once again, five-star hotels are quite pricey but well worth it.

491. While Handcuffed to Your Bed at Home

So you've tried being handcuffed to the bed at the five-star hotel. Now it's time to bring the kink home. It may be a little personal but you can do it.

BEST POSITION Cowgirl for him and Deck Chair for her

PROS It's a lot cheaper that going to a hotel every time you're feeling kinky.

CONS Be careful not to scratch the bed!

492. While Blindfolded in a Room Full of People

Having sex in front of other people is a good way to release your inhibitions. Adding a blindfold in a weird way makes you feel more secure because you can't see others watching you.

BEST POSITION Missionary or Deep Stick

PROS It's a great way to relax and let go.

CONS Make sure that you're with people that you trust to avoid any unexpected incidents.

493. In a Room Full of People—Without the Blindfold

Now that you're feeling more comfortable, try it without the blindfold.

BEST POSITION Missionary or Deep Stick

PROS You'll actually feel more in control without the blindfold.

CONS You have to let go of any insecurities about your body and being naked.

494. In a Suite of a Fancy Hotel Room

Not ready for the hand cuffs? Can't afford a five-star hotel? Then spring for the nicest hotel that you can afford and make it a goal to see how many sheets and towels you can destroy on a wild weekend romp.

BEST POSITION Anything goes!

PROS Lots of women feel more comfortable experimenting and letting go when away from home. It's not "real life" after all, it's vacation!

CONS He'll probably ask why you don't act that way at home.

495. In the Stairwell of That Fancy Hotel

There's just something really raw about having sex in the stairwell of a fancy hotel. You can get really freaky in your room, in the elevator, and in the stairwell.

BEST POSITION Dancer or Bodyguard

PROS High-end hotels, like high-end department stores, are more forgiving of their guests' activities.

CONS It's still a stairwell, so comfort is nonexistent.

496. In Front of Your Hotel Window with the Curtains Open

Strip naked, open the curtains and have sex right up against the window. If anyone sees you, they'll likely clap and cheer!

BEST POSITION Bodyguard or Dancer

PROS You're away from home, so it's unlikely you'll see anyone you know.

CONS Another hotel guest may complain but so what? They shouldn't be looking in your window.

497. In the Spa During a Couples Massage

It's a little more difficult to find but if you look, you can find certain massage parlors that will do couples massages with happy endings. It brings a whole new meaning to mutual masturbation!

BEST POSITION Manual Stimulation

PROS It's like cheating with your partner in the room.

CONS It's not for everyone. Many people will have to overcome some serious inhibitions to go through with it.

498. In a Recording Studio

Have sex in a recording studio and take home your own private soundtrack as a souvenir.

BEST POSITION Game's On or Standing Doggy Style

PROS The sound booth is virtually soundproof so you can really let go and get loud.

CONS Unless you work at a recording studio, it may be difficult to get access.

499. While House Sitting

Some of you may not approve, but next time you're house sitting use it to your advantage. Really let loose and have sex everywhere in the house. It's like christening a new home—it's just not yours.

BEST POSITION Try them all. Look back at Chapter 1 if you get stuck.

PROS It's like being in a hotel, but you have the whole house to work with.

CONS Clean up after yourselves in case the homeowners come home early.

500. At a Public Beach in the Middle of the Day

Release your inhibitions by having sex on the beach in the middle of the day.

BEST POSITION Missionary or Spoons

PROS Enjoy the sun, the ocean, and each other.

CONS It is against the law to have sex in public, so keep your eyes open to see who's watching you and if they seem to mind.

501. In a Dark Closet

It's much easier, for women especially, to loosen up and let go in total darkness. Go into a closet with no windows and just feel your way around.

BEST POSITION Standing Doggy Style or Standing Oral

PROS You can do whatever you want. No one can see you.

CONS Put the condom on before you go into the closet because it'll be very challenging to get it on right in total darkness.

502. Fantasy or Virtual Reality Sex

There are some really cool adult virtual reality games you can play on your computer these days. These games allow you to create characters and then send these characters off on animated, 3-D sexcapades.

BEST POSITION Literally anything goes!

PROS You can literally explore ALL of your sexual fantasies in a safe role-playing environment.

CONS It's not real human sex, but you'll definitely want to rip each other's clothes off when the game is finished.

503. In a Karaoke Bar

Singing off key after you've had a few drinks isn't the only perk of hanging out in a dark karaoke bar with your partner!

BEST POSITION Game's On or Manual Stimulation

PROS It's raunchy, it's fun and it's virtually harmless. What's not to love?

CONS Karaoke bar floors—or any bar floor for that matter—are pretty dirty.

504. In a Porno Theater Booth

It doesn't get much raunchier than sex in a porno booth! Squeeze in and have fun.

BEST POSITION Standing Doggy Style or Game's On

PROS It's porn and real sex at the same time.

CONS Most porn is geared to men, so if you're a man take a few minutes to find out what she wants. A happy and satisfied woman is a very giving woman!

505. In an Adult Toy Store

If you can't get any creative ideas in a toy store, then maybe it's time for a therapist.

BEST POSITION Standing Doggy Style or Game's On

PROS Just remember that all leather items are nonrefundable.

CONS Toy stores will not appreciate your playing with the merchandise before paying and it is actually illegal to have sex in a toy store.

506. In a Raunchy Dive Bar

Sure, upscale bars are great fun, especially to have a little sexual fun in. However, there's nothing like dirty sex in a raunchy dive bar!

BEST POSITION Dancer or Game's On

PROS It's a fun and exciting way to go a little outside the box and get dirty with your partner.

CONS You might lose your partner in the crowd.

507. On the Rooftop of a High-Rise Building

Get away from it all by heading up to the roof. It can even be fun to try some kinky new sex positions or games that you won't normally try in your own home.

BEST POSITION Missionary or Cradle

PROS Being up on the roof can help you let go of some of your inhibitions. It's very freeing to be up that high.

CONS Rooftops vary greatly from rooftop parks to rooftop maintenance areas, so you'll need to work with what you've got.

508. In a Room Full of Mirrors

This one is really good for women! We're all so judgmental of our bodies and perceived imperfections. Get naked and have sex in front of the mirror. Watch your every move and enjoy how sexual you really are.

BEST POSITION Try them all.

PROS It's a private, yet safe way to explore being exposed and voyeuristic at the same time.

CONS Finding a room full of mirrors. You can use your own bathroom as a good starting point.

509. In a Huge Empty Lecture Hall

The acoustics in a lecture hall are very similar to a large cave. Moan and scream and let it all out.

BEST POSITION Mastery or Lap Dance

PROS Release your inhibitions and be verbal during sex.

CONS If you're too loud, you'll attract building security.

510. In a Huge Lecture Hall During a Lecture

You won't be able to get into very many positions, but during a boring slideshow when the lights are low, one of you can get on the floor and give the other one some great manual or oral action.

BEST POSITION Game's On or Manual Stimulation

PROS It's a great way to get through a boring lecture.

CONS Make sure you don't attract too much attention or the presenter will wonder why everyone's looking at you instead of the slideshow.

511. In a Public Jacuzzi with Other People

It's unlikely that anyone else will know if you are just pretending or doing the real thing. Let them guess!

BEST POSITION Mastery or Lotus

PROS It's a pretty safe way to enjoy some public sex.

CONS Water is not a lubricant.

512. In a Lifeguard Chair Overlooking the Ocean

Enjoy the incredible view of the ocean from the lifeguard chair. Do this one at night so that you don't draw unwanted attention.

BEST POSITION Mastery or Lap Dance

PROS It's a good way to have sex at the beach without getting sand in every crack and crevice.

CONS You are limited to just a few positions and if you get too wild, you could fall out.

513. On the Set of a Movie

Get into character and act out some the sexiest movie scenes that you can think of. It can be anything from romance to porn, just have fun with it.

BEST POSITION It really depends on the movie set and the scene you are acting out.

PROS You can let go of you inhibitions because you're in character and it's not *really* you.

CONS Unless you know someone, it may be challenging to sneak onto the set. Maybe take a tour and get lost.

514. Theme Room of the Madonna Inn

There are so many different theme rooms at this inn in San Luis Obispo, California, that you can get really creative. There's everything from a safari room to an English tea room. Find one that fits your mood and go for it!

BEST POSITION Anything goes!

PROS Immerse yourself in a different environment for a few days and see how sexual you can really get with your partner. It's the perfect time to try new things.

CONS You may find out about some secret fantasies (yours or your partners) that you really didn't want to know.

515. At One of the FantaSuite Hotels

From the ancient land of Caesar's Court to the futuristic Space Odyssey, let the FantaSuite Suites transport you to the world of your dreams. Each suite is a unique experience, an adventure, a romantic retreat designed to completely immerse you in the getaway of your choice. Check it out at *www.fantasuite.com.*

BEST POSITION Anything goes, it depends on the furniture in the room!

PROS They have these in several states.

CONS Trying to choose a theme.

516. In the VIP Room of a Swinger Club

Do you like to watch or like to be watched? Even if you've just been playing with the idea in your head, this is the perfect place to let go and just be. There's no pressure to do anything and at the same time, there's no judgment if you do. Next time you're in Dallas, make sure to check out Iniquity, Dallas's finest couples-only lifestyle club. Dance, play, or just watch! Check it out at *www.iniquityclub.com*.

BEST POSITION Missionary or Mastery

PROS It is a great place to watch and explore your fantasies.

CONS Not all clubs are as nice as Iniquity, so do your research and pick one that fits your needs and desires.

517. At a Private Swinger Party (House Party)

Check out a few clubs first because most of the people who attend private house parties already know the ropes. Just be honest with the host and participants about what you're looking for and they'll be happy to help.

BEST POSITION Anything goes!

PROS Couples in the swinger community are normal people and are happy to educate and inform.

CONS House parties can be a little more risqué than what you'll see at a club.

518. At Swingfest

There's no better place to let go and have some crazy sexy fun than at Swingfest, the world's largest swingers party and adult expo. Everyone else is there for the same reason! Check out the website to see where this year's Swingfest is being held: *www.swingfestevents.com*.

BEST POSITION Anything goes!

PROS It's the perfect place to REALLY let go.

CONS Don't do anything that you'll regret later. Remember, everything that you do in public may be videotaped by someone else.

519. During Spring Break

The next best thing to Swingfest is spring break! While not as private—Swingfest rents out an entire hotel—it's still a very common place to let go and go a little crazy.

BEST POSITION Anything goes!

PROS It's another good place to *really* let go.

CONS This is where the idea for *Girls Gone Wild* came from! So be careful what you expose in public.

520. At a Local Dungeon

While we're on the topic of releasing your inhibitions, do you have any secret bondage, domination, or submission fantasies? It can be challenging for a curious couple to explore these waters on their own, in their houses. If you check around, you can find a good teacher in your area.

BEST POSITION Anything goes, except for boring missionary sex!

PROS Check out some of the public or private dungeons in your area. Most people in these communities are more than happy to answer all of your questions and get you started on the right path.

CONS You'll have to let go of your preconceived ideas and go into it with an open mind.

521. At a Hotel with an Hourly Rate

This is cheesy, cheap, and dirty. Sweet! Meet your partner at a sleazy hotel with an hourly rate for a lunch time romp.

BEST POSITION See how many different positions you can do in one hour.

PROS You don't have to be "proper" in a sleazy hotel.

CONS Cleanliness is a concern; you may want to bring your own blanket to put over the bed.

522. At a Private BDSM Club or Party

BDSM (bondage, discipline, dominance, submission, sadism, masochism) involves a varied and complex set of activities in which participants voluntarily take on different roles that may or may not be sexual in nature. Like the swinger parties, you can legally do more at home than you can at a club. Get to know the party hosts before attending a party so that you know what you're getting yourself into.

BEST POSITION Anything goes!

PROS Private parties can be smaller and more intimate, so you can get personal attention and instruction.

CONS Some people allow themselves to be pressured into doing things that they later regret. Establish your boundaries before you get involved in the first place.

523. At a Halloween Party in Full Costume

There's no more relaxing way to let go and have fun than behind a mask. A mask seems to give people more confidence than a bottle of Tequila.

BEST POSITION Mastery or Standing Doggy Style

PROS It's like having an affair with your partner.

CONS Make sure that you wear an easy access costume that is not difficult to get in or out of.

524. Underneath Her Enormous Hoopskirt at a Halloween Party

What a great way to enjoy a party. Find one of those costumes with the huge hoop skirt. Stand in the middle of the room while your man gives you oral under the skirt. See if you can keep a straight face!

BEST POSITION Standing Oral

PROS It's a good way to have some public sex without getting naked.

CONS Sorry boys. This one's just for her.

525. Fellatio under a Table with a Long Tablecloth

See if you can keep a straight face while your partner goes down on you under the table. Take turns to see if the waiter figures it out.

BEST POSITION Game's On

PROS It's a fun and sexy thing that you can do pretty safely in public.

CONS Don't look at the floor in most restaurants. You may lose your appetite.

526. On an Outside Bed at Your Favorite Seaside Resort

More and more hotels are putting real beds on the beach these days. They're great for simply lounging around or exploring your sexually adventurous side.

BEST POSITION Missionary or Cowgirl

PROS It's way better than sex on a beach towel.

CONS You're on a public beach, so there's a risk of getting ticketed or arrested.

527. At a Rave

Raves are raunchy and fun places to really let your inhibitions go. If you've never been to a rave, check one out!

BEST POSITION Dancer or Bodyguard

PROS Everyone minds his/her own business at a rave. It's all about just letting loose!

CONS There may be lots of drugs and alcohol and people that are too young to be consuming them.

528. In a Photography Studio

Hire a professional photographer to take some really sexy photos. If you look, you can find one that will photograph you having sex. These will be cherished memories for a very long time.

BEST POSITION Anything goes!

PROS It's a safe environment to let go of some of your inhibitions around sex and your body. Professional photographers can find a good angle for anyone!

CONS You'll have to get over your stage fright.

529. While Being Photographed by an Open-Minded Professional Photographer

If you're not ready to go to a photography studio, then opt for bringing a photographer to your home. It's a totally different experience. You can even practice in front of a close friend without any film in the camera.

BEST POSITION Anything goes!

PROS You'll be more relaxed in your own home than in a professional studio.

CONS The lighting and effects may not be as good as they would be in the studio.

530. In Front of Your Personal Private Video Camera

Okay, baby steps. Set up your video camera on a tripod and have sex in front of it. Just don't be too hard on yourselves if the angle is not quite right and the lighting is off. That's what the pros are good at.

BEST POSITION Anything goes!

PROS You can be as romantic or as pornographic as you like.

CONS The quality will not be as good as a professional can produce.

531. While Being Videotaped by Your Open-Minded Friend

Okay, here's the next baby step. Get your good friend Joe to come over and film you. It's still not professional quality, but it's the next step from the tripod.

BEST POSITION Anything goes!

PROS He can move the camera around and really have some fun with it.

CONS Make sure that Joe gives the tape back when he's finished so it doesn't end up on YouTube.

532. At an Upscale Restaurant

There's nothing like having sex in a stuck-up restaurant and getting away with it! Have your partner sneak under the table for a "dropped fork" and give you oral or vice versa. Nothing is more taboo than doing something dirty in a fine, upscale restaurant!

BEST POSITION Game's On or Dancer

PROS Taboo equals inhibition in our book. Break the taboos. Release the inhibitions.

CONS While the wait staff might not say anything, it is sometimes easy for the other diners to notice.

533. At a Nude Beach During the Day

There's no better place to get over your hang-ups around being naked than to walk down a nude beach during the day.

BEST POSITION Missionary or Dancer

PROS You'll realize that no one has a perfect body and that it's okay.

CONS Pure nudists will not approve.

534. On Stage

Get up on stage and have sex. Turn on the lights and feel what it's like to be in the spotlight.

BEST POSITION Missionary or Deck Chair

PROS Again, this section is about releasing inhibitions— it *should* make you feel a bit uncomfortable.

CONS You'll need access to a stage. This is easier for some than others. It just depends on your connections.

535. On Stage with an Audience

This is your graduation. If you look around, you can find some underground "sex theaters" where people get up on stage and perform (or pretend to perform) sexual acts in front of an audience. Just do it!

BEST POSITION Cowgirl or Cradle

PROS If you can do this, you have graduated.

CONS Are these theaters legal? Probably not.

536. On Top of a Huge Speaker with the Bass On (Howard Stern Style)

It's the sex act made famous by Howard Stern. Turn the speaker on its side and get on top. Have your partners make various noises into the microphone and see which ones feel the best. And yes, you can both do it—not just the girl.

BEST POSITION Cowgirl or Lotus

PROS It's a fun way to play with sound and vibration.

CONS Not everyone can orgasm by vibration alone, but you can have fun trying.

537. Right Next to Someone Who Has Had a Little Too Much to Drink and Is Out Cold

Having sex with someone else in the bed can be very exciting. It's a little safer if you know they're passed out and won't wake up.

BEST POSITION Missionary or Spoons

PROS This is another idea that makes most of us uncomfortable—someone else in the room while we're having sex. This way you can try it while they're sleeping.

CONS They may wake up and want to join you.

538. Sex with a Stranger at an Anonymous Costume Party

This one may be a bit much for most, but it doesn't get much more erotic than having sex with a total stranger, someone you'll never know or ever see again.

BEST POSITION Bodyguard or Standing Doggy Style

PROS It's a chance to explore a secret fantasy.

CONS Always practice safe sex and make sure that your partner is okay with this.

539. At a Strip Club

Most women shy away from strip clubs and get jealous when their man goes without them. Well, in most cases it's because the woman is too insecure to go herself. Get over your insecurities and join your man at the strip club and buy him a lap dance and buy yourself one too!

BEST POSITION Game's On or Dancer

PROS You can even give your man a lap dance!

CONS You can't touch the girls, but you can touch each other!

CHAPTER 15

KINKY FREAKY PLACES

As you read the following places you may find yourself thinking, "Okay, that's just weird!" The following places are intended for those of you who like things a little kinkier than most and just a little left of normal.

540. With a Prostitute in a Seedy Hotel

Get Kinky Freaky by adding a third person who is a professional. Just do your research and work with a licensed agency that has a good reputation.

BEST POSITION Anything goes!

PROS It's a great way to try a threesome without worrying about the emotional baggage that comes later.

CONS She's a prostitute, and it's illegal in most places.

541. With a Blow-Up Doll at a Bachelor Party

Blow off some steam by humping the blow-up doll at a Bachelor party. Take lots of pictures, you won't want to forget this!

BEST POSITION Missionary or Standing Oral

PROS It's all in good fun!

CONS You might like it.

542. During a Sex Magick Ritual

Sex Magick can be as simple or as complicated as you want to make. It can be as easy as setting an intention when you orgasm to a full-blown magick ritual.

BEST POSITION Missionary or Deep Stick

PROS Sexual energy is a very powerful force. That's why so many magick rituals include some form of sexual activity or byproduct.

CONS You can inadvertently invoke energies that you did not intend to. It's worth reading up on this stuff and working with a knowledgeable instructor.

543. During a Conjugal Visit in a Prison

Make your next visit something to remember.

BEST POSITION Missionary or Cowgirl

PROS Being away from your partner while he or she serves time is not easy. At least this will give you something to remember until your next visit.

CONS Your partner is still in prison!

544. At Shibaricon

Shibaricon is the world's premier international pansexual annual exhibition and conference that focuses on education and information exchange of erotic Japanese rope bondage (*www.shibaricon.com*).

BEST POSITION Anything goes!

PROS You'll get to learn about the art of rope bondage from professional instructors and even get to experience it yourself if you like.

CONS Where do you tell the babysitter you're going?

545. At a Friend's Party While Hypnotized

If you're the type of person who is susceptible to hypnosis, this could be an interesting way to let go of some of your inhibitions that are keeping you from having an incredible sex life.

BEST POSITION Anything goes!

PROS Hypnosis from a certified professional can work wonders!

CONS A friend's party may not really be the best place for this. How about in the office of a professional hypnotherapist?

546. At an Abandoned Airfield

This is a great kinky way to remember this nostalgia of World War II. To get the most of this scene it's important to find proper costumes for this era. A typical role-play scenario would be to pretend that the airfield has just undergone a significant bombing and you are the only two survivors.

BEST POSITION Dancer or Delight

PROS This is a great way to really explore the scene as well as your role within it. Really get into it.

CONS It may be difficult to find an abandoned airfield that's not protected by the military.

547. In a Baby's Playpen

We've all seen the diaper episodes on Jerry Springer. But this fetish is more common than you might think. Not ready for diapers? Why not test your boundaries by having sex in a baby's playpen.

BEST POSITION Doggy Style or Cradle

PROS It's a safe way to test boundaries in the privacy of your own home.

CONS Baby playpens were not made to hold adults and may not support your weight.

548. In a Bat Cave

Get on the Batman costume, get on the Cat Woman costume and go for a romp in the bat cave. It may not be as clean and high tech as the one in the movies, but it will be an adventure.

BEST POSITION Dancer or Standing Doggy Style

PROS It's truly unique and interesting.

CONS Bat guano—otherwise known as Bat Poop!

549. In a Bathtub Full of Grapes

From the words of Mae West, "Peel me a grape!" Seriously, having sex in a bathtub filled with grapes, peeled or otherwise, is a fun way to experiment with food. Use the green seedless ones for easy cleanup because the red grapes may actually stain your tub.

BEST POSITION Cowgirl or Cradle—the important thing is to roll around in the grapes

PROS Grapes are a safe food to experiment with because they make a minimal mess.

CONS Cost and cleanup. It's not exactly cheap to fill your bathtub with grapes and someone will have to scoop out all of the grapes when you're finished.

550. In a Tub Full of Shaving Cream

Not ready for the grapes? Try some shaving cream. It's less expensive and easier to clean up. Go buy ten to twenty of those cheap ninety-nine-cent cans of shaving cream. You can have fun spraying it all over each other or you can fill the bathtub and then get in.

BEST POSITION Cowgirl or Cradle

PROS It's just fun!

CONS It can be messy to clean up, but that's what the shower is for! And be careful—shaving cream is slippery.

551. In a Dark Alley on the Seedy Side of Town

A dark alley is a great place to let go of inhibitions and explore your darker side. There are dark, creepy, and often forbidden places. Fear is a great aphrodisiac. Perfect!

BEST POSITION Dancer or Standing Oral

PROS It's a great place to let go of inhibitions.

CONS Your fear maybe justified—you could be in real danger. So watch your surroundings.

552. In a Dark Corner of a Haunted House

Sneak off into a dark corner of a haunted house and have some fun while everyone else is running scared. If you plan it properly you can even make your escapades part of the act.

BEST POSITION Dancer or Standing Oral

PROS Remember, fear is a great aphrodisiac.

CONS It might be difficult to slip away from the group. The flow through haunted houses is usually very well defined. Try going through the house a couple times first to get your bearings and spy out dark corners.

553. In a Dog Kennel

It can be your private kennel in your home or the dog run at a boarding kennel. The private option allows you to take your time and play with a leash and collar. Try not to weird out the dogs!

BEST POSITION Doggy Style or Standing Doggy Style, of course

PROS What a great way to explore your primal instincts, like dominance and mating.

CONS If you work at the boarding kennel, you may get fired.

554. In the Cemetery on a Dark, Foggy Night

What could be creepier?

BEST POSITION Standing Doggy Style or Missionary

PROS If you're into the whole fear/sex thing, this should do it for you.

CONS Who else is running around the cemetery on a dark foggy night?

555. In a Dr. Seuss–Themed Hotel Room

Indulge your inner child and book a Dr. Seuss-themed hotel room and really let your inhibitions go. Where? Loews Portofino Bay Hotel at Universal Studios. You can do it in the house with a mouse, in a box with a fox. You get the idea.

BEST POSITION Try several positions but the point here is to have fun with it.

PROS This is really a great way to get in touch with your inner child.

CONS The Dr. Seuss-themed rooms start at just over $600 per night for two adults—ouch!

556. In a Dumpster

This one may be a challenge for many of you. Not because it's kinky, but simply because it's dirty, it's nasty, and it smells.

BEST POSITION Standing Oral or Standing Doggy Style

PROS This one will definitely get you outside of your box.

CONS Let's face it, it's just filthy and you'll definitely need a shower when you're done.

557. Behind a Dumpster at Your Apartment Complex

Well, this is better than *in* the dumpster. If you just can't wait and the only thing around is the dumpster, then have at it!

BEST POSITION Standing Doggy Style or Dancer

PROS It's very doubtful that anyone will look for you there.

CONS You may have to fight for position with the stray cats and mice.

558. On the Set of a Really Creepy Movie

If you get the chance to tour the movie set of your favorite horror movie, it's a great opportunity for some freaky sex.

BEST POSITION Anything goes—depending on the movie and the set!

PROS It's a fun and new way to enjoy your favorite horror movie.

CONS Don't break the set. Much of the furniture is made of cardboard or cheep wood.

559. In a Ghost Town

There's something a little freaky about ghost towns, but they are a great place to stop on a road trip to get a quick bite and enjoy a quickie!

BEST POSITION Cowgirl or Deck Chair

PROS Another great opportunity to push your boundaries.

CONS While there might not be actual ghosts, the local law enforcement may not appreciate your sense of adventure.

560. Inside of a Huge Air Duct

It may not be kinky freaky, but it's definitely unusual. These are the kind of air ducts and air conditioning ducts that run through most corporate buildings, retail stores, and restaurants.

BEST POSITION Missionary or Drill

PROS Bragging rights. How many of your friends have tried this one?

CONS Not only is it difficult to find these larger ducts, you'll actually need a screwdriver and even a ladder to get into most of them.

561. In the Jail Cell of an Old Prison

Take the tour of an old prison like Alcatraz Island and sneak off into one of the old cells, or even the execution room, for a bit of naughty, spine-tingling fun. Find an old jail bed or even the electric chair and use these props to your advantage to get down and dirty.

BEST POSITION Bodyguard or Standing Doggy Style

PROS The implied danger is that you have to sneak past the tour guides to make this happen. It's so exciting!

CONS Many of the cells and execution rooms on these tours are often locked or protected by glass windows. But you can always opt for a quickie in the bathroom.

562. In a Mental Hospital

Try an abandoned mental hospital like you see in the movies. Or try to find your way into a padded cell of a modern mental hospital. What a great place for rough sex. You can throw each other around and no one gets hurt!

BEST POSITION Butterfly or Standing Doggy Style

PROS This is a safe place to release some of your inhibitions and explore some rough sex. Throw in a straitjacket and it becomes bondage play!

CONS You may like it so much you want to do it again and again and again.

563. In the Morgue

Whether you have sex on the table or inside a cold chamber (doors open please), having sex in a morgue can be quite an adventure.

BEST POSITION Butterfly or 69

PROS The feel of cold hard steel against your naked bodies can be quite exciting.

CONS It's very likely that there will be actual dead bodies in the same room with you.

564. On a Pile of Stuffed Animals

Bring back the kid in you and make love to your partner in a big pile of stuffed animals! Taking a trip back to childhood in a very adult way can be extremely interesting both physically and emotionally, especially if they're your own childhood toys.

BEST POSITION Missionary or Cowgirl

PROS This is a great chance to release some of your adult inhibitions.

CONS Lots of little beady eyes staring at you while you have sex.

565. At the Tattoo Parlor

There's a very fine line between pain and pleasure. Now's your chance to really blur those lines. While sex is not recommended during the process (you'll end up with a really bad tattoo), try having sex immediately after the process while the pain is still fresh in your mind.

BEST POSITION Dancer or Standing Doggy Style

PROS You'll find the sexual experience to be more intense because of the tattoo procedure.

CONS It's doubtful the owners will actually let you have sex in the chair or on the table, but you can ask.

566. In an Abandoned Building

With the recent downturn in the economy, there are abandoned corporate buildings all over the place. It doesn't have to be a condemned building. It could even be in an office building that's up for sale.

BEST POSITION Bodyguard or Dancer

PROS It's incredibly arousing to be the only ones in the entire building.

CONS Breaking and entering is a crime, so try a more creative approach, like getting permission.

567. At a Random Construction Site

It can be a house, restaurants, or foreign office building. The important differentiator between this and an abandoned building is that the construction is incomplete. There's no wallboard; there is no carpet. It should feel rough and hard to your senses.

BEST POSITION Standing Oral or Standing Doggy Style

PROS Picture buff construction workers and the tool girl from *Tool Time* on the old sitcom *Home Improvement*.

CONS Construction sites are by definition not safe places to hang out, so be careful while you're on site.

568. Bungalow 3 in the Chateau Marmont

This is the room where John Belushi overdosed and died. Bungalow 3 is a beautiful room with its own private garden. It might be a little creepy considering the history of the room, but if you're into that sort of thing it can be a fun and interesting way to get down with your partner.

BEST POSITION Missionary or Deep Stick

PROS It's a beautiful and glamorous hotel on Sunset Blvd.

CONS It's a bit pricey with rooms starting around $350 per night.

569. Room 105 in the Highland Gardens Hotel

Visit a piece of American history by holing yourself up in the room where Janis Joplin died when she overdosed on heroin at the Highland Gardens Hotel in Hollywood, California.

BEST POSITION 69 or Cowgirl

PROS It's a fun and different way to experience a piece of American history.

CONS This is not a luxury hotel so set your expectations appropriately.

570. During a Peep Show at an Adult Video Store

Make the peep show more enjoyable by giving oral to your partner while they enjoy the show.

BEST POSITION Lap Dance or Game's On

PROS It's like watching porn—live.

CONS You'll most likely have to pay double since there are two people in the room.

571. In the Back of a Police Car

Hop in the back and have some criminal sex while your friend the cop drives with the sirens on. You could even handcuff each other to the car. You'll have to have a good connection to make this one happen but it'll be great fun!

BEST POSITION Cowgirl or Deck Chair

PROS If you're going to have sex in a car, do it right in a police car!

CONS Finding the cop who's willing to play along.

572. In the Dark Depths of a Gold Mine

You've hit the mother lode! Gold glitters in your lover's eyes when you take them into the gold mine for something extra special and sensual.

BEST POSITION Bodyguard or Standing Doggy Style

PROS It has the same appeal as a bat cave without the bat guano.

CONS It might be hard to break away from the tour without your guide noticing.

573. In the Haunted Suite of a Haunted Hotel

Give yourself a little scare by taking your partner to a haunted hotel, a real one! Snuggle up together and wait and see if any of the ghosts make their presence known.

BEST POSITION 69 and Spoons

PROS Fear is a great aphrodisiac.

CONS Haunted typically means old, so you may miss out on some luxuries that you're accustomed to.

574. In the Kitchen Wearing a Sombrero and Slathered in Refried Beans and Sour Cream

This is food play at its best, assuming you like Mexican food. Put down some painting tarp on the floor and cabinets and have fun eating, licking, and just getting out of your comfort zone.

BEST POSITION Spread Eagle or Standing Oral

PROS This is a yummy treat.

CONS The cleanup!

575. In the Playroom of a Local Swinger Club

You don't have to have sex with anyone else, but there's something incredibly erotic about watching other people have sex. It's way better than Playboy porn.

BEST POSITION Butterfly or Missionary

PROS A safe and encouraging environment to really let out your inner pervert.

CONS Surprise pictures and video footage that may come out later when you run for office.

576. In the Timberline Lodge

Give yourself a scare by getting a little randy in the same hotel that the famous movie *The Shining* was filmed, the Timberline Lodge, Oregon. It's fun, creepy, and thrilling all at the same time.

BEST POSITION Bodyguard or Dancer

PROS Fear is a great aphrodisiac.

CONS You may get so freaked out that you just want to go home.

577. Make Your Own Porno at a Professional Studio

Make your own porn flick. You'll be able to enjoy it for years to come. You can do it yourself with a camera and tripod, but you'll miss out on some great angles, zooming, and panning that you'll get with a professional behind the camera.

BEST POSITION Definitely try them all.

PROS It's a great opportunity to release your inhibitions.

CONS Your friend may never look at you the same again.

578. In an Abandoned "Haunted" House

Remember that creepy old house down the street that all the kids swore was haunted? Revisit those childhood memories and break through the fear by having sex in that old house.

BEST POSITION Mastery or Drill

PROS It'll be a really fun and exciting adrenalin rush.

CONS Abandoned houses can be dangerous so be careful. And don't forget that breaking and entering is against the law.

579. At an Abandoned or Empty Rail Car Yard

Sneak into an empty box car for some adventurous sexual play. If you get lucky, maybe there will be an empty locomotive.

BEST POSITION Missionary or 69

PROS Having sex in a new environment is not only necessary but exciting as well.

CONS On site security.

580. In an Ax Murder House

Having sex in a house where actual murders took place can be spine-tingling to say the least. One of the most popular cases is the Villisca Axe Murders of 1912 (*www.villiscaiowa.com*) where two adults and six children were found brutally murdered in their beds in the small Midwestern town of Villisca, Iowa.

BEST POSITION Spoons—so that you can stay close together!

PROS A very high creepiness factor.

CONS A very high creepiness factor.

581. On an Old Civil War Battlefield

That is an awfully big cannon! You can be sure and give those old civil war heroes a good show by getting down and dirty at a Civil War battlefield.

BEST POSITION Cowgirl or Missionary

PROS It's a great opportunity to do a *Gone with the Wind* re-enactment.

CONS Some might interpret having sex on a Civil War battlefield as disrespectful. Go with your gut on this one.

582. In an Old Deserted Mansion

Take it up a notch from the old haunted house down the street and find an old deserted mansion. It doesn't have to be haunted, just deserted. You're probably not the first to try it there!

BEST POSITION Try a different position for each room.

PROS It's bigger than that old house so there's more to explore.

CONS An old mansion may have a groundskeeper, so be careful not to get caught.

583. On Abandoned Railroad Tracks

Near that abandoned rail yard, you're likely to find some abandoned railroad tracks. Take turns tying each other to the railroad tracks or explore your more primal side.

BEST POSITION Cradle or Mastery

PROS You will have great adventurous sex.

CONS Comfort, or lack thereof—rocks, wood, and railroad ties. Ouch!

584. On Stage at a Deserted Underground Theater

Underground theaters have it all: open-minded people, incredible amateur acting, and an often deserted stage, especially during the day. Make love together in the middle of the stage.

BEST POSITION Missionary or Lotus

PROS Public sex in a private way is a good way to get your exhibitionist groove on without too much exposure.

CONS You may get caught.

585. Under a Highway Overpass

Nestle in between the concrete below a highway overpass and get your blood flowing louder than the cars above you. It's a great way to steal a quickie in the middle of a road trip!

BEST POSITION Dancer or Deck Chair (if you have a soft blanket)

PROS It's a great place for a quickie.

CONS Be wary of passing cars (especially police cars).

586. In a Deserted Swimming Pool

Neighbor refinishing the pool? Public pool closed for remodeling? It's the perfect opportunity to "go off" in the deep end.

BEST POSITION Cowgirl or Standing Doggy Style

PROS It's a whole new perspective.

CONS The cement is hard so bring a blanket.

587. Underneath the Hornet Spook Light

Legend has it that the bright ball of orange light that appears every single night at this locale is the spirit of two Indian lovers who committed suicide together. Check it out in the Devil's Promenade in Hornet, Missouri, right at the Oklahoma state line.

BEST POSITION Lotus or Dancer

PROS Finally, a good reason to go to Oklahoma.

CONS It's literally in the middle of nowhere! We're talking dirt roads here.

588. At Scarborough Fair

Get into costume and step into the sixteenth century at the Scarborough Renaissance Festival just south of Dallas, Texas. There are plenty of places to step into or behind for a quickie.

BEST POSITION Standing Doggy Style or Dancer

PROS Don't you just love all of those busty costumes!

CONS Some of the Shakespearean clothing is difficult to get on and off, so you might have to settle for unzipping only.

CHAPTER 16

BEST PLACES TO LOSE YOUR JOB

Sex in the workplace is very common whether you want to admit it or not. Here are some great ideas to spice it up a bit. Just an FYI—if you get caught, you'll probably get fired.

589. On the Copier

This one's a little cliché, but you'll have some really interesting souvenirs to take home. Set the copier for color and have fun.

BEST POSITION Standing Doggy Style or Delight

PROS You'll have souvenirs to take home.

CONS Positions will be difficult and you may damage the copier.

590. On the Company Forklift

Not to be confused with a "Tallahassee forklift." If you or your partner works at a construction site or even in a warehouse, you can make the most of it by having sex in one of the forklifts.

BEST POSITION Spread Eagle on the lift part or Mastery in the cab

PROS Turn an ordinary day at the construction site into something fun and risqué!

CONS Sex on the lift can be dangerous. Wear a hard hat.

591. On the Roof of Your Office Building

If you work in a high-rise office building, head up to the roof. You'll be amazed at the number of places to have sex—looking out over the horizon, behind an air conditioning unit, and even on a ledge (please look for an enclosed ledge).

BEST POSITION Dancer or Cowgirl

PROS It's a good place to get away from your coworkers.

CONS It's probably not protected from the weather, so it may be obvious where you've been.

592. On Your Desk at Work

This is perfect if you have an office and can lock the door. If not, just wait until after hours when no one else is around.

BEST POSITION Butterfly or Standing Doggy Style

PROS In your own office, you can lock the door.

CONS You may not get much work done.

593. At a Business Conference with a Coworker

Come on. We all know someone who's had an affair at a business conference. You may even be one of them!

BEST POSITION Anything goes!

PROS You're out of town and it just seems like the perfect place to enjoy a one-night stand.

CONS Sex with your coworkers is always a bad idea!

594. After Hours at Work, on Your Boss's Desk

You know you want to. It just feels so wrong but so right, especially if you don't like your boss. Besides, his or her desk is probably bigger than yours.

BEST POSITION Butterfly or Standing Doggy Style

PROS Your boss's desk is probably bigger than yours, and the door probably locks.

CONS If you get caught, you will most likely be fired. Maybe you want to get fired—and what a way to go!

595. After Hours at Work, on Your Boss's Sofa

Why not take it to the next level and get comfortable. If your boss has a really big office, then he or she will most likely have a nice comfy sofa as well.

BEST POSITION Missionary or Mastery

PROS It's way more comfortable that the desk or floor.

CONS Because it's more comfortable, you're likely to get caught in a really compromising position—clothes off and spread around the room.

596. During Working Hours under Your Boss's Desk

This is an especially fun idea if you're dating your boss or maybe you can come up with an excuse to sit at your boss's desk for the afternoon. Then you can have your partner join you, under the desk.

BEST POSITION Game's On

PROS This is a less obvious way to fool around at your boss's desk. Assuming of course that you can keep a straight face.

CONS The biggest concern is if your boss needs to get something out of the desk while you're there.

597. In Your Boss's Car While Running Errands

This is just too easy! While you're out running errands in your boss's car, stop by and pick up your partner for a quickie in the car. Just make sure to actually run the errands!

BEST POSITION Mastery or Deck Chair

PROS It's a great opportunity for a midday quickie.

CONS If your boss finds out, you'll likely get fired, unless he sees the value in a midday quickie.

598. At Your Boss's House with Your Boss's Wife

Definitely want to get fired? Have sex with your boss's wife at your boss's house and then send him the video.

BEST POSITION Her favorite position—the idea is to get back at your boss.

PROS It'll go down as the best way to get fired!

CONS He may actually hunt you down and shoot you! It's called a crime of passion.

599. During Working Hours under Your Own Desk

Don't want to risk it with your boss? Why not let your partner hide under your desk or in your cubicle? It's the same idea only a little less risky.

BEST POSITION Game's On

PROS You have more control over your work environment than your boss's.

CONS You may not have as much room under your desk.

600. During Work Hours Behind the Reception Desk

Does your partner work at the reception desk? You can tease your partner all afternoon from under the desk or if it's a slow day, you can just bang each other right there!

BEST POSITION Game's On or Standing Doggy Style

PROS It's just erotic and sexy.

CONS Your partner may lose his or her job. Oh well, there are always other jobs.

601. Under the Desk in Your Neighbor's Cubicle

Fooling around in your neighbor's cubicle when he or she is on vacation could mean less chance of getting caught by someone looking for you.

BEST POSITION Game's On or Spread Eagle

PROS At least it's not your desk.

CONS Is it really any different?

602. At Your Boss's Christmas Party on the Bed

Same old boring Christmas party? Not this year. Sneak into the master bedroom for a quick romp in the bed. At least if you get caught, you can claim that you had a little too much wine.

BEST POSITION Butterfly or Doggy Style

PROS It'll be adventurous and slightly risky.

CONS If it's a nonalcoholic Christmas Party, you won't have an excuse.

603. In the Supply Closet at Any Boring Office Party

This is a great way to have fun at a boring party. Slip into the supply closet for an office quickie.

BEST POSITION Dancer or Bodyguard

PROS It's an office party—they'll just think your went back to work.

CONS Hopefully you don't get caught by someone looking for more napkins.

604. In the Control Room of a Television Studio

If you work in a TV studio, you can definitely have some fun in the control room after everyone else has left for the rest of the day! Just make sure not to get caught on camera or to push the wrong button and make your escapades a public affair.

BEST POSITION Delight or Standing Doggy Style

PROS It's dark and the doors lock.

CONS Lots of buttons and switches that may accidentally get tripped.

605. In the Employee Lounge

Claim a headache or indigestion from lunch and slip away to the employee lounge for some afternoon delight.

BEST POSITION Butterfly or Delight

PROS There are normally comfortable sofas for your enjoyment.

CONS You may not be able to lock the door. Oh well, if you get caught you can inform your audience that you're working to cure your headache.

606. In the Ladies' Room

It's quite easy to sneak away to the ladies' room for some office sex.

BEST POSITION Standing Doggy Style or Dancer

PROS You're already in the ladies' room, so freshening up afterward is a snap.

CONS Women are more easily shocked than men, which could be an issue if you get caught.

607. In the Men's Room

The men's room is another alternative, but as a general rule, the ladies' room smells much better! But if you get caught, a man may be a little more understanding of the situation.

BEST POSITION Standing Doggy Style or Dancer

PROS Men generally have fewer sexual hang-ups and are less likely to tattle if you get caught.

CONS Men's rooms are typically not as nice as ladies' rooms.

608. In the Parking Garage of Your Office Building

If you have a parking garage in your office building, it's a great place for a quickie right after lunch. Just stay in your car and enjoy your dessert.

BEST POSITION Cowgirl or Deck Chair

PROS You're already in your car.

CONS You can really wrinkle your work clothes in the car due to the limited space.

609. In the Stairwell of Your Office Building

Now you have a new reason to take the stairs! Stick to the higher floors because you'll run into fewer people at that level.

BEST POSITION Standing Doggy Style or Dancer

PROS Your clothes will get less wrinkled than in the car.

CONS Dirt and grime. You'll be better off sticking to standing poses so that you don't go back to work with stair stripes on your back.

610. In the Janitor's Closet

We've already mentioned the supply closet when talking about office parties, but don't overlook the janitor's closet. It will get less traffic during normal work hours.

BEST POSITION Dancer or Bodyguard

PROS You can have some interesting fun with the brooms.

CONS Watch out for harsh chemicals.

611. In the Walk-In Cooler of a Restaurant

It may be a bit chilly but a walk-in cooler can make for a wonderful sex stop. If you work at a restaurant, it's fairly easy to steal a moment in the walk-in cooler especially in the early morning before the restaurant opens.

BEST POSITION Bodyguard or Standing Doggy Style

PROS It's fairly private.

CONS It also quite chilly.

612. In the Office Kitchenette

Working late? Need a pick-me-up? Instead of reaching for a cup of coffee, put your partner up on the counter or table for a sexual pick-me-up.

BEST POSITION Butterfly or Spread Eagle

PROS It's way better for you than coffee.

CONS You may not be the only ones working late.

613. On the Office Waiting Room Sofa

This idea is really good if you work in an office where you see clients. These types of offices normally have comfortable waiting rooms for clients. Make sure that you're the last ones out of the office, and make a quick pit stop in the lobby before you lock up.

BEST POSITION Delight or Drill

PROS Adds a new level of customer service to your office.

CONS There's a high risk of getting caught by a coworker who forgot something or by the janitor.

614. On Your Conference Room Table

How many boring meetings have you had to sit through at work at that conference table? Give yourself something fun to remember at the next conference by having raunchy sex on the table, under the table, and all around the table.

BEST POSITION Butterfly or Standing Doggy Style

PROS The conference room has lots of options for different positions.

CONS Unfortunately, few of the surfaces are actually comfortable.

CHAPTER 17

BEST PLACES TO FEEL ONE WITH NATURE

With our busy schedules and hectic lives, we often forget to just stop and breathe. Spending time in nature allows us that time, it helps us remember what's really important in life, and it heals us. All of the places in this section will help you reconnect with nature while enjoying your partner at the same time.

615. In a Hedge Maze

Lose yourselves in the world's largest hedge maze located on the Dole plantation in Hawaii.

BEST POSITION Missionary or Cowgirl

PROS Be one with nature.

CONS Don't literally get lost. Make sure you know how to find your way out of the maze.

616. In an Outdoor Hot Tub Overlooking the Ski Slopes

If you're tired of hanging out in the lodge by the fireplace, then venture to the outdoor hot tub to reconnect with nature and for some hot steamy sex.

BEST POSITION Mastery or Delight

PROS Being in a hot tub surrounded by snow is incredible.

CONS Other couples may join you, but that's only a con if you don't want them to.

617. In an Amphitheater

Having sex in a theater is fun, but an amphitheater will put you and your partner in touch with your creative sides as well as nature!

BEST POSITION Missionary or Spoons

PROS It's an outdoor way to enjoy a show and each other.

CONS There's a chance of getting caught and escorted off the premises.

618. At a Mystery Spiritual Energy Vortex

There are several sites across America that claim to be spiritual or energy vortexes. Probably the most common is Sedona, Arizona, where spiritual teachers and followers gather to enjoy this area of highly concentrated spiritual energy. See how this energy brings you together as a couple sexually.

BEST POSITION Lotus or Mastery

PROS Whether or not you believe in spiritual energies, it can't hurt to give it a try.

CONS Be wary of all the spiritual teachers wanting to heal you. As with all intensely spiritual things, there are real healers and show healers.

619. Christmas Tree Farm in the Trees

There's something sexy and sensual about shopping for the perfect Christmas tree. Lying on the ground, underneath a snow-covered Christmas tree; snuggle up for a deliciously romantic and sensual romp in the snow.

BEST POSITION Missionary or Spoons

PROS This one might be worth getting caught.

CONS It's cold outside so bundle up.

620. In a Cave Hotel

Take your lover spelunking and see how interesting it can be in a secluded dark spot inside the earth. A cave hotel is more hotel and less cave, but it's still underground.

BEST POSITION Anything goes!

PROS You can enjoy being underground and still enjoy the comforts of being in a hotel.

CONS These types of hotels tend to be very touristy.

621. At the Casitas De Gila Guesthouses

Strand yourselves in the velvety silence of the high desert's Casitas de Gila, a civilized, cliffside oasis Near Silver City, New Mexico. Relax, unwind, and simply enjoy each other. Check it out at *www.casitasdegila.com*.

BEST POSITION Anything goes!

PROS It's a great way to turn up the heat and break the ice with a new partner.

CONS It's in the desert, so don't get lost.

622. Archaeology Dig

The best place to have sex on an archaeology dig is probably in a remote area in your Jeep. You might not find any dinosaur bones, but it will be less of a disappointment if you've gotten naughty with your partner before the dig ends.

BEST POSITION Doggy Style or Cowgirl

PROS You'll never have so much fun digging in the dirt.

CONS Sand. It has an amazing way of getting into every crack and crevice.

623. Arkansas Ouachita National Park During a Long Cross-Country Drive

Drive off the highway at any Ouachita exit and find a road leading to the park. Not many people there and it's beautiful. Roll down the windows and listen to the sound of nature.

BEST POSITION Cowgirl or Deckchair

PROS Great diversion from the long drive, you might make it four more hours!

CONS Car seats can leave marks on your legs.

624. On a Sailboat 100 Miles from Shore

Rent a sailboat and sail out 100 miles, bring lunch, sun block, and plenty of cold water along with your lover and a blanket.

BEST POSITION Drill or Lotus

PROS The silence, the ocean, and the privacy.

CONS Make sure sun block covers *all* parts.

625. On a Nude Beach at Night

It's one thing to have sex on the beach, but if you really want to get in tune with nature, you need to be *au naturale* yourself.

BEST POSITION Dancer or Doggy Style

PROS It's a great way to release any inhibitions about your body and sexuality.

CONS Hard-core nudists may not appreciate what you're trying to do.

626. On a Pontoon Boat in the Middle of the Lake

Day or night, there's something about being on the water that is very exhilarating. Maybe it's the sun, or the scantily clad people running around everywhere—but enjoy floating around.

BEST POSITION Cowgirl and Missionary

PROS Being naked in the sun is incredible arousing.

CONS There's a real chance of sun burn and bug bites.

627. During a Guided Boat Tour on a Scenic River

Enjoy a guided boat tour on a scenic river. Find a quiet place on the boat for a quickie. If it's quiet, you may even be able to do it right on deck.

BEST POSITION Standing Oral or Dancer

PROS Enjoy each other and a scenic river ride, all at the same time.

CONS The boat could be crowded. Find out when it's the off-season and book your tour then.

628. In a Glass-Bottom Boat

Watch the fish swim by as you enjoy a sexual encounter in the boat.

BEST POSITION Doggy Style or Rear Entry

PROS It's a great way to see nature without having to get in the water with it.

CONS Most glass-bottom boats come with tour guides and lots of other people.

629. While Diving in the Ocean

You'll have to pick a warm water location so that you don't need diving suits, but there's no way to get closer to the fishes than having sex underwater.

BEST POSITION Standing Doggy Style or Bodyguard

PROS Buoyancy! It's almost like being weightless so those few extra pounds will matter a little less.

CONS Buoyancy can also be a con—the water will provide little resistance, so you'll need to pick a position where you can hold on to each other and create your own rhythm.

630. Inside a Butterfly House

Let the butterflies flutter around you as you and your partner experience each other in an entirely new way and celebrate the gift of life and rebirth. Be very careful that you're not destroying any of the sanctuary's plant or animal life!

BEST POSITION Missionary or Lotus

PROS Connecting with nature and celebrating life and rebirth can be an incredible experience.

CONS Be careful not to disturb the natural habitat.

631. In a Cactus Garden

Cacti are one of the only plants that survive in the desert. At a cactus garden, you'll be able to see many different varieties of cacti, and while you're at it, you can really get a good look at your partner too.

BEST POSITION Missionary or Doggy Style

PROS What a great way to experience a little style of the old southwest!

CONS Don't have sex touching a cactus plant or you might get stuck somewhere you don't want a thorn.

632. In a Canoe under the Stars

We've talked about having sex in a canoe while going down the river, but what about floating on a peaceful lake? You'll still have to worry about tipping over, but there will be much more time to lie back and gaze at the stars.

BEST POSITION Mastery or Deep Stick

PROS It can be very romantic.

CONS You're still in a canoe and limited by stability and space.

633. While Camping in an Underground Cave or Cavern

Take your sleeping bags and spend the night in an unoccupied cave or cavern. Snuggle up and get cozy.

BEST POSITION Missionary or Spoons

PROS Enjoy the privacy and be one with nature.

CONS Bears—make sure the cave really is unoccupied.

634. In a Convertible with the Top Down Parked on a Secluded Dirt Road

No caves nearby? Rent a convertible and head out of the city until you find a dirt road. Drive down the dirt road until you find a good place to park. Put the top down and enjoy being in the county and looking at the stars.

BEST POSITION Mastery or Doggy Style

PROS It's one of the easier ways to connect with nature and requires less commitment than a camping trip.

CONS The farmer who lives down that dirt road may not be a romantic as you are.

635. In a Corn Maze

Get lost in each other's arms in the middle of a corn maze! It's the perfect place to get a little down and dirty in the middle of nature without anyone noticing!

BEST POSITION Missionary or Deck Chair

PROS It's really easy to find a corn maze around Halloween.

CONS You'll likely be trespassing on private property, so be careful not to get caught.

636. At the Edge of a Steep Cliff at Sunrise or Sunset

Enjoy the romantic scenery of a sunrise or sunset over a cliff with your sweetheart. It's the ultimate romantic way to say "I love you!" Make sure you have a blanket with you to lie on, because cliffs can be quite rocky!

BEST POSITION Lotus or Standing Doggy Style

PROS You can experience breathtaking views and take your partner's breath away all at the same time.

CONS You're outside so plan accordingly for weather, bugs, etc.

637. In a Field of Snow

Assuming you live somewhere where it actually snows, this should be quite simple. And it's beautiful and romantic.

BEST POSITION Missionary or Spoons

PROS Snuggling in the sleeping bag.

CONS Brrr ... It's friggin' cold!

638. In a Field of Wheat at Noon in the Summer Beside a Very Well-Traveled Road

Bring a blanket, lie down in the wheat, and strip naked. It's hot and you're sweaty, but who cares? Take this time to get in touch with your inner country boy/girl.

BEST POSITION Missionary or Cowgirl

PROS You can hear the cars going by but giggle because you know they can't see you.

CONS It's dirty and hot.

639. In a Cornfield

Drive through Middle America in the summer and you'll have plenty of cornfields to choose from.

BEST POSITION Missionary or Standing Doggy Style

PROS The corn is much taller than wheat.

CONS The dirt and heat.

640. In a Field of Daisies

This is a slightly more romantic twist on the wheat field. Find a field of daisies, or whatever your state flower is and literally roll around in the flowers.

BEST POSITION Missionary or Cowgirl

PROS It's very romantic.

CONS Let's hope you're not allergic.

641. In a Gazebo at the Park in the Moonlight

Visit the park after midnight when everyone else is home asleep. You'll have privacy and can enjoy the romance of being naked in the moonlight.

BEST POSITION Dancer or Mastery

PROS Naked skin in the moonlight is a beautiful sight.

CONS If you're in a public park, make sure to watch out for the local law enforcement.

642. In the Soft Grass with No Blankets

St. Augustine is a place where you can find nice soft grass, but pick your own favorite spot. Get naked and discover the feeling of the cool grass on your bare skin.

BEST POSITION Missionary or Cowgirl

PROS Rolling in the soft grass. Need I say more?

CONS Chiggers and spiders also like soft, cool grass.

643. In a Hawaiian Rainforest

Imagine being alone with your partner in the middle of a tropical paradise, with just you and nature. Remember your animal side and get primal.

BEST POSITION Standing Doggy Style or Dancer

PROS The beauty of the rain forest.

CONS There can be some crazy insects, animals, and plant life in a rain forest, so don't stray too far off the beaten path.

644. On an Indian Reserve in the Wild

Being on an Indian Reserve is all about being close to nature and making love is something that is sacred to many Indian tribes.

BEST POSITION Missionary or Cowgirl

PROS It's an opportunity to get spiritual and commune with nature.

CONS Make sure that you're not violating any sacred spaces.

645. On an Indian Reserve in a Teepee

Many public campgrounds offer teepee rentals to help you get in touch with nature. You can sit around the camp fire, or dance naked, whatever it takes to get tuned in to your surroundings.

BEST POSITION Anything goes as long as it's in your teepee!

PROS It's better than sneaking around in the woods.

CONS You're camping, so the little luxuries like a shower may not be available.

646. On an Inflatable Fun Island in the Middle of a Lake

In many ways this is more fun than a boat. You can bounce around and dive in the water any time you feel like it. It also feels closer to nature because you're truly floating and drifting.

BEST POSITION Anything you can do in a bed

PROS It's like a waterbed in the middle of the lake.

CONS Don't forget to anchor or you may end up on the other side of the lake.

647. In a Koi Pond

Whether you have a koi (goldfish) pond in your backyard or you're using a friend's, slipping in and doing it among the fish is a whole new experience!

BEST POSITION Mastery or Delight

PROS You can get close to nature in your own backyard.

CONS Koi are nasty, dirty fish, so be careful and take a shower afterward!

648. In a Giant Indoor Aquarium

Get really up close and personal with the fishes in a giant indoor aquarium.

BEST POSITION Bodyguard or Dancer

PROS The fish won't mind. They may enjoy watching the show for once instead of being the show.

CONS The water is cold!

649. In a Pile of Fall Leaves in Your Backyard

Nature's own mattress can make a wonderful love nest for two. After you're finished raking the yard, jump in and let the autumn games begin.

BEST POSITION Missionary or Spread Eagle

PROS Everyone loves playing in the leaves.

CONS That includes all of the bugs in your backyard.

650. In a Sleeping Bag under the Stars

You don't even have to leave home. Just take a sleeping back in the backyard or even on an upstairs deck and snuggle up together on a cool fall or spring evening.

BEST POSITION Missionary or Spoons

PROS Snuggling together naked in the sleeping bag is a real plus.

CONS The hard ground—maybe bring and extra sleeping bag for padding.

651. In a Tent on a Camping Trip

If you love the outdoors, there's just something about being in nature at night with just a tent between you and all the critters skittering around outside. With the crickets and tree frogs singing, the experience can really get you in touch with nature and with your primal side.

BEST POSITION Missionary or Spoons

PROS It's out in the middle of nowhere—and therefore very private. What more could you ask for?

CONS Bugs, twigs, rocks, dirt—beware of these things! Keep your tent zipped at all times, and you'll avoid most of the creepy crawlies.

652. In a Tidal Pool

Tide pools offer wave after wave of ocean water crashing against rocks and the shoreline. Let your passion crash again and again in a tidal pool!

BEST POSITION Mastery or Delight

PROS The waves create an incredibly sensual rhythm. Try to match them with your bodies.

CONS Sharp rocks—make sure to wear your water shoes.

653. In a Wild Animal Sanctuary

Wild animal sanctuaries are a bit like zoos, but geared more toward the animals than the patrons gawking at them. Take advantage of this natural setting by doing it like the animals do.

BEST POSITION Missionary or Doggy Style

PROS It's more *one with nature* than sex at the zoo.

CONS There really are wild animals roaming around, so keep your eyes open.

654. In an Apple or Peach Orchard in the Summer

Peaches and apples are the food of summer memories. Now you can create summer memories of your own by getting frisky with your partner underneath a peach tree in a quiet orchard on a sunny afternoon.

BEST POSITION Missionary or Dancer

PROS What a romantic and sexy way to spend a hot, summer afternoon!

CONS Watch out for the same stuff you would if you were having sex anywhere outside—sticks, rocks, bugs, etc.

655. In a Hot Spring

Swimming holes are great, but are often limited to summertime weather. Why not get a little freaky in a hot springs in the fall or winter?

BEST POSITION Standing Doggy Style or Dancer

PROS The warm water will feel different than the normal chilliness of other swimming holes.

CONS Be very careful of the illegal hot springs. These can be too hot to swim in. Always make sure there is a sign that says it's safe to swim.

656. Underneath a Moonbow

A moonbow is like a rainbow, only under the light of the moon instead of the sun. It happens when the placement of the moon and a waterfall are just right. Even though it happens rarely, it's a magical sight! Cumberland Falls, Kentucky, is a common place for a moonbow sighting!

BEST POSITION Missionary or Spoons

PROS It's beautiful and romantic.

CONS The conditions have to be just right for a moonbow to form, so you may have to make a few attempts to get the scenery just right.

657. Underneath a Natural Arch

Natural arch formations are some of the greatest ways to experience nature at its very best. Get sexy and sensual with your partner underneath one for a totally new experience.

BEST POSITION Missionary or Dancer

PROS It can be extremely romantic to settle down underneath a natural arch and experience each other sexually in a way that you never have before.

CONS Watch out for rocks and lizards.

658. At a Volcano Retreat

Make love while the fires of passion burn at a sensual volcano retreat. It's hot, erotic, and definitely a huge turn-on. Get ready for your own eruptions.

BEST POSITION Dancer or Standing Doggy Style

PROS Nothing is hotter than an active volcano! It's super sexy and even a little dangerous.

CONS It's dirty and hot—but is that really a negative? Also, there's a small chance the volcano will erupt while you're there. But that's not enough to stop you, is it?

659. At the Bottom of the Grand Canyon

Enjoy lying on your backs and looking up at the incredible vistas of the Grand Canyon.

BEST POSITION Missionary or Bodyguard

PROS How can you beat having sex at one of the Eight Wonders of the World?

CONS Watch out for the same stuff you would if you were having sex anywhere outside—sticks, rocks, bugs—oh, and tour guides.

660. At the Top of the Grand Canyon

Enjoy having sex overlooking the Grand Canyon especially at sunset.

BEST POSITION Missionary or Bodyguard

PROS You'll have easier access to the top of the canyon than the bottom.

CONS It's not as private as being nestled at the bottom of the canyon.

661. In Your Backyard When It's Raining

Next time it's raining (not storming), put on some very sheer clothes and run around in the rain. If you're not aroused by the time your clothes are clinging all over your bodies, then you really need to examine your life because something's just not right!

BEST POSITION Bodyguard or Standing Doggy Style

PROS Very erotic opportunity to connect with nature and with one another.

CONS You may get a little chilly but the excitement will override any chill you may feel.

662. In a Conservatory or Botanical Garden

Enjoy walking through a conservatory filled with fragrant flowers and incredible plant life. Stopping to make love can turn an ordinary conservatory tour into something extraordinary!

BEST POSITION Missionary or Standing Doggy Style

PROS The beautiful plant life will stir your senses.

CONS It's very public, so be careful that you don't get kicked out.

663. On a Deserted Nature Trail at Your Local State Park

Go hiking at a state park and take a break in the bushes for some great nature sex. Find a tree to lean on or a bush to hide behind.

BEST POSITION Standing Doggy Style or Dancer

PROS Enjoy getting one with nature at it's best—in the middle of a beautiful state park.

CONS Watch out for park rangers.

664. In a Fragrant Rose Garden

Nothing smells as sweet as a rose, just watch the thorns! A rose garden makes for a wonderful place to make love. If it's your private rose garden, sacrifice the roses and lay the petals all over the ground to make a soft, fragrant bed.

BEST POSITION Missionary or Cowgirl

PROS The softness and sweet smell of the rose petals will add romance to your adventure.

CONS Watch all those prickly, sharp thorns. They hurt!

665. On a Golf Course

There are literally hundreds of places on the golf course for a quick rendezvous with nature. Slip behind a tree, duck into a sand trap, or enjoy the soft grass on the green.

BEST POSITION Missionary or Cowgirl

PROS Golf courses are well manicured so there'll be less chance of burs, thorns, or unwanted wildlife.

CONS Golf courses are very busy, so it's better to wait until nightfall.

666. In an Igloo

An igloo is basically a small dome built with blocks of hardened snow. Ideally you'll find an igloo that's already been built!

BEST POSITION Missionary or Spoons

PROS You'll stay relatively warm in the igloo.

CONS If you have to build your own igloo, you may be too exhausted to have sex. Maybe in the morning you'll have the energy to enjoy the fruits of your labor.

667. In a Snow Cave

A snow cave is not the same thing as an igloo; a snow cave may be easier for most of us to come by. All you need is a deep snow bank. Have fun playing in the snow while you make your snow cave and then take your sleeping bags inside to snuggle and do whatever else comes to mind.

BEST POSITION Missionary or Spoons

PROS Snow caves are actually quite warm and cozy.

CONS If you don't build a snow cave properly, you can suffocate or it may collapse, so do your research first.

668. In the Desert

Deserts are extremely dry. Quench your thirst by making your partner a little wet on a road trip or just an excursion to a desert. You can admire the beauty of the desert and the beauty of each other's bodies in the middle of nowhere. How romantic and sensual!

BEST POSITION Missionary or Cowgirl

PROS For those of us who like to be warm, this is a much better option than a snow cave.

CONS Try to avoid getting hot desert sand in the places that matter.

669. In the Forest in the Rain

If you've ever been in the forest during a rain shower, it's absolutely incredible. Everything is so green and lush, and the smell is so clean and refreshing.

BEST POSITION Missionary or Cowgirl

PROS It doesn't get more romantic and sensual than this.

CONS After the rain stops, the mosquitoes come out.

670. In the Ocean While Snorkeling

Total freedom of movement allows for some exceptional sexual moments. The sea allows you to do things not possible on dry land.

BEST POSITION Standing Doggy Style or Bodyguard

PROS Being naked in the middle of a coral reef, making love to your partner, is thrilling and romantic.

CONS There are things that bite and sting in the water.

671. In Your Own Vegetable Garden

Sneak outside to your vegetable garden and lie down in between the rows of squash and zucchini. No one will ever look for you there!

BEST POSITION Missionary or Cradle

PROS It's a fun way to bond with the garden that you worked so hard to grow.

CONS You might end up crushing a few plants.

672. On a Mountain Peak with Cloud Mist Surrounding You

Get into mountain climbing and reward yourselves with incredible sex above the clouds. Mountains peaks in the U.S. range from easy to difficult. You should be able to find one near you that fits your energy and skill levels.

BEST POSITION Missionary or Cowgirl

PROS Looking down at the clouds is incredible.

CONS You have to climb a mountain first. Or you could get creative and have a helicopter take you to the summit—but that's cheating.

673. In a Mudslide

You can try this in one of two ways: 1: you can fill your bathtub with a concoction made of rum, Kahlua, and Irish cream, or 2: you can put a big pile of dirt in your backyard and soak it with water. Either way, when the mixture is complete, take off all your clothes and wrestle in the mud.

BEST POSITION Dancer or Doggy Style

PROS Whichever option you choose, you're bound to have tons of fun.

CONS Whichever option you choose, you'll have a big mess to clean up.

674. Take an ATV into the Mountains

Nothing is as breathtaking as the view from a mountain top. Take your lover with you for the added enjoyment while exploring mountain peaks in an all-terrain vehicle.

BEST POSITION Mastery or Lap Dance

PROS You can experience total isolation—just you the bears and the mountain lions.

CONS Bears and mountain lions live in the mountains.

675. During a Paintball Game in the Woods

There's nothing like getting all dressed up in camouflage and sneaking off to the woods to get paint splattered all over you, or how about a little role play? Let him take you prisoner and have his way with you, or vice versa. Body painting sounds more fun to me! Visit Elma Paintball in Elma, Washington. You can find more info at *www.emeraldcityhobbies.com*. This is a great place to try out some paintball fun!

BEST POSITION Standing Oral or Standing Doggy Style

PROS It's a great opportunity for some role play.

CONS Does shooting each other count as getting one with nature? Oh well, at least you're out in the woods.

676. During an Airsoft Game in the Woods

Airsoft is similar to paintball, but the participants shoot at each other with pellets that do not explode paint all over you. Don't you just love the idea of taking each other prisoner?

BEST POSITION Standing Oral or Standing Doggy Style

PROS It's a great opportunity for some role play.

CONS Getting paint all over you is the best part of this type of activity. This just seems painful.

677. In an Empty Stall of a Petting Zoo

This is getting one with nature in a different way. If you're not easily bothered by farm animals, a roll in the hay at the petting zoo of the county fair can be a great place for a quickie.

BEST POSITION Doggy Style or Deck Chair

PROS The animals won't mind.

CONS The smells can be fairly overwhelming at times.

678. Next to a Campfire

There's nothing more romantic than lying together naked by a crackling fire. Get one with nature by making it a campfire.

BEST POSITION Cowgirl or Spoons

PROS The fire will keep you warm and cozy.

CONS The hard ground is not quite as comfortable as a bear skin rug.

679. Next to a Train Track

Lay your sleeping bag next to a train track and feel the ground vibrate as the train rushes by. Just don't get so close that you get hit by debris coming off the train.

BEST POSITION Missionary or Spoons

PROS The intense sound and vibration of the train creates an effect similar to that of being in a thunderstorm.

CONS Just watch out for typical outside stuff like hard ground, rocks, and bugs.

680. On Top of a Frozen Pond in the Middle of Winter

Slide your sleeping bag out to the middle of the pond and listen to the sounds of nature while you make love. Just make sure the pond is frozen solid—you wouldn't want to fall in the icy water.

BEST POSITION Missionary or Deck Chair

PROS It's very peaceful and serene.

CONS Brrr . . . it's cold.

681. One Hundred Miles Out in the Middle of Nowhere

It doesn't matter where you go so long as you're totally in the middle of nowhere. Make sure there are no cars, no houses, absolutely no sounds of urban life.

BEST POSITION Anything goes!

PROS There is no better way to be one with nature.

CONS No indoor plumbing for 100 miles.

682. In an Outdoor Shower

Whether at the lake or in your own backyard, explore the exhibitionist in you while having sex in an outdoor shower.

BEST POSITION Dancer or Standing Oral

PROS Being naked in the shower together is awesome!

CONS Nosy neighbors—but they get what they deserve.

683. Outdoors, in the Sun

The sun is a natural aphrodisiac so take advantage of this and spend some time together naked in the sun. A nudist beach is the perfect place to experience the sun on your body.

BEST POSITION Anything goes!

PROS The feeling of the warm sunshine on your naked body is incredible.

CONS You'll have to overcome your shyness.

684. On an Airboat in a Florida Swamp

If you really want to be one with nature, take an airboat to the middle of a Florida swamp. It has an incredible ability to make you feel small and insignificant compared to the nature around you.

BEST POSITION Mastery or Standing Doggy Style

PROS You get to experience the deafening silence of nature.

CONS Big mosquitoes and big snakes—and let's not forget the crocodiles.

685. On a Picnic Table

Don't forget your picnic basket for an afternoon delight! Picnics are romantic in and of themselves and adding a randy sex session on the picnic table will make it even better!

BEST POSITION Standing Doggy Style or Butterfly

PROS It's a great way to experience nature without going too far from home.

CONS Unless you lay your blanket on top of the table, you might get splinters in some unwanted areas.

686. On a Blanket of Pine Needles

One of the best things about Christmas time is the smell of pine. Take a walk into a pine forest and make a bed of pine needles. Pile them high for a soft aromatic bed and then lay a blanket across the pine needles so they don't poke your skin.

BEST POSITION Missionary or Cowgirl

PROS The smell of pine and being surrounded by nature will invigorate your senses.

CONS You may have to work a little to make your soft bed.

687. On a Raft Floating Down the River

Enjoy the passing scenery on a big, soft raft. This is a clothing optional event.

BEST POSITION Missionary or Mastery

PROS It's very peaceful and serene.

CONS Watch out for sunburn and mosquitoes.

688. On a Sailboat in the Middle of the Lake

Imagine just the two of you on the deck of a sailboat. Drop anchor and enjoy!

BEST POSITION Standing Doggy Style or Mastery

PROS Privacy—you can go anywhere you want.

CONS If you don't know how to sail then you'll need a captain.

689. In a Field of Sunflowers

Enjoy some summer fun while looking up at the sunflowers overhead.

BEST POSITION Missionary or Cowgirl

PROS You'll get a whole new perspective while looking at Sunflowers from underneath.

CONS If it's summer, it will be hot!

690. On the World's Largest Sycamore Stump

Have sex on a giant tree stump to tune in to nature and history. Visit Kokomo, Indiana, and have sex against the World's Largest Sycamore Stump.

BEST POSITION Dancer or Standing Doggy Style

PROS It's the biggest tree stump in America.

CONS It's a tree stump—watch out for ants and splinters.

691. Under a Natural Waterfall

This is straight out of many TV commercials and romance novels. If you haven't had sex under a waterfall yet, it's time to check this one off your list!

BEST POSITION Dancer or Standing Oral

PROS It's like a natural shower only with the force of nature behind it.

CONS The water is cold! Opt for behind rather than under a waterfall.

692. Underneath a Grapevine in a Vineyard

Large vineyards are all over the country. How romantic! Turn an ordinary wine-tasting tour into something incredible.

BEST POSITION Missionary or Deck Chair

PROS Get a whole new perspective while looking at the grapes from underneath.

CONS Grapes are going to be all over the ground. Without a blanket, you'll return to your tour covered in purple stains and obviousness!

693. Underneath a Meteor Shower

Certain times of year are better for this but if you listen to the news, you'll know when the next big meteor shower should occur.

BEST POSITION Missionary or Lotus

PROS Its nature's fireworks.

CONS In Texas, most meteor showers peak at 4:00 A.M., so it means getting up really early—do some research on your area and see what you can expect from your adventure!

694. Underneath the Northern Lights

The Northern Lights are one of the greatest spectacles that America has to offer. Get sensual with your partner underneath the lights for a romantic getaway.

BEST POSITION Missionary or Spoons

PROS It's very beautiful and romantic.

CONS If you can see the Northern Lights that means it's probably cold outside, so bundle up.

695. On Top of a Warm Boulder

If the Northern Lights are too cold, experiment on a warmer surface. While hiking near a lake or river find a large, warm boulder to lie on for an afternoon tryst.

BEST POSITION Delight or Dancer

PROS Think of it as a hot stone massage with a happy ending.

CONS Boulders can actually get hot, not just warm, so be careful.

696. While Hiking in the Woods

Hiking is great fun and a wonderful way to exercise. You can stop along the way near a tree or on a large rock for a quickie, or find a more secluded nook for a long, sensual and romantic interlude.

BEST POSITION Missionary or Doggy Style

PROS Sex while hiking is both spontaneous and invigorating. You're already hot and sweaty, so really let loose and be one with nature. Do it like the animals do.

CONS Bug bites and poison ivy are never fun, especially on parts that are not normally exposed!

697. While Ice Fishing

Learn how to keep warm while ice fishing by taking your lover with you on a trip and snuggling up together in an ice fishing shack.

BEST POSITION Dancer or Mastery

PROS It's a new way to experience fishing.

CONS The smell of fish and bait can turn a lot of people off.

698. While Rolling Down a Hill Together Slowly

Find a gentle sloping hill covered with thick grass, or even better, a thick blanket of snow. You don't have to roll at breakneck speed. Just gently roll, taking turns who's on top. (You can practice rolling on your living room floor and then take it outside!)

BEST POSITION Missionary and Cowgirl

PROS It's a fun way to change positions.

CONS Watch out for rocks and sticks.

699. While Snow Skiing

While skiing down the slopes, take a short detour. Finding a suitable position with skis on might be difficult to do, so consider taking your skis off to allow you and your partner a little more flexibility.

BEST POSITION Standing Oral or Standing Doggy Style

PROS The mountains are beautiful.

CONS Don't stop on a slope that seems unstable. You wouldn't want to go sliding down the mountain with your pants down!

700. During a Hail Storm

Nothing says adventure like the fury of Mother Nature! Find cover for your head and then enjoy the rest of the storm in ecstasy.

BEST POSITION Dance or Bodyguard

PROS Fierce storms are just sexy.

CONS Make sure you're safe from the hail; if it's big enough, it can kill you.

701. During a Tornado in the Storm Shelter

Run for the shelter and then have incredible sex while your adrenaline is still flowing.

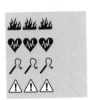

BEST POSITION Dance or Bodyguard

PROS Fierce storms are just sexy.

CONS The only truly safe shelter from a tornado is underground, but if you have to die in your closet, this is the way to go.

702. During a Hurricane

Board up the windows and let your passion rage with the storm outside.

BEST POSITION Missionary or Cowgirl

PROS Hurricanes are one of the best examples of the pure energy of nature. Take this opportunity to embrace your pure sexual energy.

CONS If you need to evacuate, please do so. You can have sex later.

CHAPTER 18

POPULAR BUT CLICHÉ PLACES

These are the places that we've all heard of more times than we care to count, and for most of them, we are left with the feeling of "why?" But who knows, one of the totally cliché places may resonate with you. You never know until you try it!

703. On a Bare Waterbed Mattress

Just add a little baby oil and slip, slide, and slither all over each other. Just remember that baby oil is not a water-based lubricant and will break down latex condoms—yes they will break! So wash the baby oil off before actually having intercourse.

BEST POSITION Manual Stimulation or Game's On

PROS It's very moisturizing for your skin.

CONS It's incredibly messy and the cleanup near impossible.

704. In a Bed with Satin Sheets

Satin sheets are nice and all, but sometimes they're almost too slippery! Give me some ultra-high thread count Egyptian cotton sheets any day!

BEST POSITION Anything goes!

PROS Satin sheet are incredibly erotic—tickle you lover's body from head to toe with the satin.

CONS You may slide right off the bed. Seriously, this has happened before!

705. At the Motel 6 While Wearing Edible Underwear

This is cheesy sex at it's best. You get edible underwear at just about any condom, lingerie, or adult party store. Meet your party for a risqué lunch date at the Motel 6 or other inexpensive motel.

BEST POSITION Spread Eagle or Oral Therapy

PROS It's a unique twist on the same ol' lunchtime quickie.

CONS Edible underwear usually doesn't taste all that great.

706. While Covered with Your Favorite Flavor of Body Frosting

Now this is more like it. Find a flavor you really like and lick that off!

BEST POSITION Spread Eagle or Oral Therapy

PROS You actually get to enjoy a flavor that you really like.

CONS Food play can be quite messy.

707. In a Bathtub Full of Jell-O

What is it about and Jell-O that makes people want to wiggle around in it? And this is a better option than baby oil. It's still a lot of fun and your condoms will be safe.

BEST POSITION Mastery of Cradle

PROS If you're choosing between baby oil and Jell-O— go with Jell-O because the cleanup is a lot easier.

CONS Jell-O can stain your tub.

708. In a Bathtub Filled with Champagne

Fill your tub with champagne and enjoy the bubbles tickling you from head to toe.

BEST POSITION Mastery or Cradle

PROS Champagne smells good and feels good on your body.

CONS It takes a few cases of champagne to fill a small tub so opt for a cheap variety.

709. In a Heart-Shaped Bathtub

The heart has long been the symbol for love. What better place, then, to show your lover a night of passion than in a heart-shaped tub? It's cliché and cheesy, but it's romantic.

BEST POSITION Mastery or Cradle

PROS If you check into the honeymoon suite you'll be treated with extra special care.

CONS Honeymoon suites with heart-shaped tubs might be too cliché for some folks.

710. On the Beach at Sunset

This one's definitely cliché but can still be enjoyable. Try to find a secluded beach so that you won't be disturbed.

BEST POSITION Missionary or Cowgirl

PROS The sunset and the waves against the shore basically define romance.

CONS Sand will get in every crack and crevice.

711. On a Bearskin Rug by the Fire

This one's in every cheesy romance novel there is, but if you give it a chance, you just might like it. Here's the scene: the warm fire, the soft rug, no TV, no cell phone, and no computer . . . just you and your lover.

BEST POSITION Missionary or Lotus

PROS It's very romantic and cozy.

CONS Poor bear.

712. On a Grand Piano

What's the fascination with this one? Yes, they did it in the movies but it just seems uncomfortable. But hey, try it anyway; you may like it.

BEST POSITION Butterfly or Standing Doggy Style

PROS You can say you did it like they did in the movies.

CONS You may damage a very expensive piano.

713. In a Cheesy Honeymoon Suite

Check in to one of those cheesy honeymoon suites where everything is over-the-top romantic. If you don't lose your dinner, you may have some really kinky sex.

BEST POSITION Anything goes!

PROS It will help you overcome some of your inhibitions and preconceived ideas.

CONS The over-the-top romance can make some people physically ill.

714. On a Huge Four-Poster Canopy Bed

Canopy beds are gorgeous and romantic. If you can find a big fluffy feather bed, even better! Have some strawberries and champagne or something else incredibly romantic to make this a night to remember.

BEST POSITION Any position you would use in a regular bed.

PROS You may enjoy it so much that you want to stay another night.

CONS Let's just hope you and your lover aren't allergic to goose down.

715. In the Spa Before a Couples' Massage

Hop on the table for a nice quickie before a relaxing massage. You can ask the massage therapist to give you ten to fifteen minutes to get ready. Trust us, it will be the most relaxing massage you've ever had.

BEST POSITION Missionary or Cowgirl

PROS Having sex before getting a massage will create an increased sense of relaxation in your body.

CONS Massage tables are pretty small, but you can raise and lower them to the appropriate height.

716. Join the Mile-High Club

This one has been at the top of the list for a very long time. Are you ready to become a member of this exclusive club?

BEST POSITION Dancer or Standing Doggy Style

PROS You can check it off your list.

CONS You'll have to do it in a small, stinky lavatory or cramped seat (unless you're in first class).

717. On a Coin-Operated Vibrating Bed

It just doesn't get more cheesy than this. You may have to make some phone calls and sneak over to the shady side of town, but there are a few hotels out there that still have operating vibrating beds. Why not try it at least once?

BEST POSITION Cowgirl or Deep Stick

PROS It's an opportunity to just let go and have fun with it.

CONS The types of hotels that have vibrating beds typically aren't the cleanest, so you may want to take your own sheets and pillows.

CHAPTER 19

SIGHTSEEING AND MORE— TOURISTY SPOTS

We're going to take you across America in a whole new way. This section will take you on an exciting and sexual tour of our great United States. It includes many of the biggest tourist areas and some that you've never heard of, but one thing is for certain, you'll never look at tour buses the same again!

718. In All Fifty States

This one may take a while, but set a goal to have sex in every state at least once. You can put a map on the wall with red stick pins for every place you've had sex. Won't that be a great conversation starter?

BEST POSITION Anything goes!

PROS You're guaranteed to have sex at least fifty times, and it's way better than collecting coffee mugs or shot glasses.

CONS It's very time consuming, but won't it be fun?

719. On the Boardwalk in Atlantic City

The Boardwalk in Atlantic City, New Jersey, provides access to hotels, resorts, shops, casinos, and more. Take a break from seeing the sights to enjoy some afternoon delight.

BEST POSITION Dancer or Bodyguard

PROS There are many places along the boardwalk for a quickie or an extended lovemaking session.

CONS You may get stuck trying to figure out where to go first.

720. At the Top of the Sears Tower in Chicago

Enjoy your lover while overlooking the skyline of Chicago, Illinois.

BEST POSITION Dancer or Bodyguard

PROS You'll get to experience the incredible view while you orgasm.

CONS It's a public place, so you may have to wait for the right time and to find the exact right place.

721. In the Gateway Arch in St. Louis, MO

The tram cars are small, cozy, and private. They scream "take me now!"

BEST POSITION Mastery or Doggy Style

PROS The view from the top of the arch is incredible.

CONS It only takes four minutes to get to the top of the arch, so you don't have much time.

722. At the Top of the Seattle Space Needle

When you get there, throw in a quick feel or a full-blown quickie!

BEST POSITION Dancer or Manual Stimulation

PROS The views are spectacular.

CONS The Space Needle wasn't exactly designed for privacy.

723. In the Alamo in San Antonio, TX

Have dinner on the River Walk. Then find a place to enjoy each other too.

BEST POSITION Dancer or Bodyguard

PROS The Alamo feels very rustic and can bring out the "pioneer" in you.

CONS The Alamo is much smaller and more crowded than you might think!

724. Onboard *Air Force One*

If you ever get a chance, how can you not? Trust me. You're not the first.

BEST POSITION Dancer or Standing Doggy Style

PROS It's the most famous aircraft in the world!

CONS Getting on board may be challenging for most of us.

725. On a Space Shuttle

Having sex in space would be really cool, but you may have to settle for being in a space shuttle on the ground. Have sex in the launch position!

BEST POSITION Mastery or Cowgirl

PROS It's a space shuttle.

CONS Once again, getting onboard could be a bit challenging.

726. On a Crowded Tour Bus

Release the exhibitionist in you by fooling around on a crowded tour bus.

BEST POSITION Game's On or Manual Stimulation

PROS Most people will be paying attention to the tour and not to you.

CONS If you take it too far you'll likely get thrown off the bus. Don't get mad at the tour guide, he's just doing his job. Your goal is to see what you can get away with before getting thrown off the bus.

727. While Having Dinner at Reunion Tower in Dallas, TX

Enjoy dinner and "dessert" at Reunion Tower—it's the big lit up ball in all the pictures.

BEST POSITION Game's On or Mastery

PROS You can enjoy views of the city during dinner and spice it up for dessert.

CONS It's a public place, so if you get too crazy your evening may be cut short.

728. At South Fork Ranch Just Outside of Dallas, TX

This was the home of JR Ewing from the TV show *Dallas* (how long ago was that, anyway?). While it's a must-see tourist spot, if you're expecting a modern-day mansion, you'll be sadly disappointed. It was a nice house when it was built, but it's not a mansion by today's standards.

BEST POSITION Missionary or Dancer

PROS Everything is bigger in Dallas.

CONS It's in the middle of nowhere.

729. At the Playboy Mansion

Now this is a mansion! It may even be a requirement: "All visitors to the mansion must have sex upon entering."

BEST POSITION Anything goes!

PROS It's the Playboy mansion and there will be hot girls running around.

CONS Hugh Hefner has agreed to open the mansion to the public, but not until he dies . . . So for now, you'll have to get an invite to attend.

730. Mountain Lake Resort, VA

Bring back the sensual and erotic romance of *Dirty Dancing* by renting a room and doing what Baby and Johnny did in the movie that was filmed at this incredible resort!

BEST POSITION Anything goes!

PROS You can experience your own version of the sensual romance and forbidden love that made *Dirty Dancing* so popular.

CONS It's a popular spot, so it can get kind of touristy in the warmer months.

731. At the Kasidie Mansion

Kasidie Mansion is a playground for swingers, hosting uninhibited parties for the hottest couples. They're located in Denver and Las Vegas, celebrating a lifestyle that people immerse themselves in. Kasidie is where people connect with new friends at an erotic, sexually charged estate.

BEST POSITION Underneath five other people as the center of an orgy on the handcrafted Italian bed in the main guestroom.

PROS You'll always hot young couples and unicorns (unicorns are beautiful single women—sorry, no solo males allowed), plenty of play areas, easy parking.

CONS The guest list is usually exclusive.

732. At Burning Man

Burning Man is a unique event that expresses the individuality of each and every person. Celebrate your intimacy! Check out the website for more information: *www.burningman.com*.

BEST POSITION Missionary or Spoons

PROS Burning Man is all about freedom of expression, so express yourself.

CONS Burning Man is not for the closed-minded, but that's not you or you wouldn't be reading this book!

733. At the Mall of America

No tour of America is complete without visiting the Mall of America (*www.mallofamerica.com*).

BEST POSITION Dancer or Standing Doggy Style

PROS It's huge. Surely you can find one place to have sex.

CONS It's huge. How do you decide?

734. In the Ladies' Lounge at Radio City Music Hall

While you're touring Radio City Music hall, the largest indoor theater in the world, located in the heart of Rockefeller Center, New York (*www.radiocity.com*), stop for a sexual break in the ladies' room and try for the largest orgasm in the world's largest indoor theater.

BEST POSITION Mastery or Lap Dance

PROS The ladies' rooms are nicer than the men's rooms.

CONS It's a public place, so step into a stall for less chance of getting caught.

735. In a Secluded Area of Bonnaroo

Bonnaroo is a four-day music and arts festival held on a beautiful 700-acre farm in Manchester, Tennessee, every June. Go for the music, stay for the sex!

BEST POSITION Missionary or Dancer

PROS Bonnaroo is an incredible festival for music, arts, and fun! You'll love experiencing each other sexually in this new, amazing environment.

CONS It is an outdoor festival, so unless you bring an RV, showers may be optional.

736. At the Great American Beer Festival

Enjoy trying several different beers and getting freaky at the same time. Visit *www.beertown.org/events/gabf/* for information on this year's Great American Beer Festival.

BEST POSITION Dancer or Standing Doggy Style

PROS Beer AND Sex—what more could you ask for?

CONS There are so many venues to choose from, try not to get stuck in the decision-making process.

737. At a NASCAR Race

If you can get pit passes, it'll be really fun to get it on at a NASCAR race. It would be even cooler to get it on in/on a racecar. Check out the schedule at: *www.nascar.com.*

BEST POSITION Dancer or Game's On

PROS You will get to experience the roar of the engines and the overall thrill of NASCAR.

CONS The smell of exhaust and burning rubber can be pretty gross. And stock cars are not built for comfort!

738. Beneath the Golden Arches, After-Hours

There's nothing more American that McDonald's. Wait until after closing when they turn the lights out and enjoy a quickie under the Golden Arches.

BEST POSITION Dancer or Bodyguard

PROS It's an American icon.

CONS This is a very public place to have sex so watch your surroundings.

739. On a Black Sand Beach in Hawaii

Not all of the beaches in Hawaii are black sand beaches, but Punalu'u beach is. Check out *www.letsgo-hawaii.com/beaches/punaluu.html* for more information.

BEST POSITION Missionary or Lotus

PROS Black sand adds a new dimension to sex on the beach.

CONS Black sand still finds its way in to every crack and crevice.

740. During a Dolphin or Whale Show at Sea World

Visit Sea World in Orlando, Florida, and enjoy some sexual fun during the whale or dolphin show. You may have to settle for some fondling in the stands or you can step out of the show for a quickie.

BEST POSITION Manual Stimulation or Lap Dance

PROS This is a good opportunity to do some heavy flirting during the show.

CONS This is really a family venue, so you'll have to keep it very mild in public.

741. With the Alligators in Gatorland

Visit Gatorland in Florida and find a secluded spot to enjoy a sexual romp.

BEST POSITION Dancer or Standing Doggy Style

PROS It's a theme park and animal reserve all in one—you should have a great time.

CONS It's an animal reserve. You may run into a real alligator if you venture too far off the beaten path.

742. In an Old West Saloon

Dress up in full character as a bank robber and saloon girl for a wild time.

BEST POSITION Dancer or Game's On

PROS Have fun enjoying the history of the wild west.

CONS Finding an operational saloon may be a challenge, but do your best.

743. On the Brooklyn Promenade, Overlooking New York City

Overlooking the city of Brooklyn can be romantic and fun, but you can add a whole other dimension to it by getting frisky.

BEST POSITION Lotus or Lap Dance

PROS Enjoy this scenic walkway on a romantic weekend.

CONS You can certainly get caught, but if you're an exhibitionist, that's just a bonus.

744. By the Confucius Statue in Chinatown, NY

This bright gold statue is really the center of Chinatown. It's incredibly hard to resist getting at least a little frisky!

BEST POSITION Mastery or Dancer

PROS Confucius was wise and so are you—wise enough to take an opportunity to publicly enjoy your partner when there is one!

CONS It's a very public street, so pay attention to your surroundings and work fast.

745. At the San Diego Zoo

Find a secluded place and pretend that you're in the jungle and get wild like the animals do. The San Diego Zoo in San Diego, California, is simply one of the best zoos in the country (according to *www.americas bestonline.com*).

BEST POSITION Dancer or Standing Doggy Style

PROS Do it like the animals do at the zoo.

CONS The smell of wild animals nearby might ruin the mood.

746. On the Hollywood Walk of Fame

Find your favorite celebrity's star and enjoy a quickie on it. Your chances of success are better at night than in the afternoon with all of the tourists running around.

BEST POSITION Standing Doggy Style or Bodyguard

PROS There are more than 2,000 stars to choose from.

CONS It's a very public spots with lots of tourists—and lots of these tourists have cameras, so be extra careful.

747. At the National Aviation Museum

Join the mile-high club on the ground by scoring with your partner at an aviation museum. Get more information on their website: *www.navalaviationmuseum.org.*

BEST POSITION Missionary or Standing Doggy Style

PROS It's a museum, so there should be lots of quiet corners and empty hallways.

CONS Try to avoid the busloads of children who are there on field trips.

748. At the Singing Dunes

California's Kelso Dunes are a good place to experience "singing dunes." If you've never heard of this phenomenon before, it's the sound that occurs when the sand moves just right—you can hear it roaring, singing, or even squeaking!

BEST POSITION Missionary or Cowgirl

PROS It might possibly be one of the coolest sex soundtracks that nature makes.

CONS You're in the desert, so it's hot, and there's lots of sand, so be careful it doesn't get into places you don't want it to.

749. At the International Spy Museum

Take a trip to the International Spy Museum, in Washington, D.C. Check it out at *www.spymuseum.org* and sign up for the Ultimate Scavenger Hunt, a fun after-hours event just for adults. You'll learn some really cool spy facts while looking for the perfect spot for a quickie.

BEST POSITION Dancer or Bodyguard

PROS Pretending to be a spy is such a turn on!

CONS It is a spy museum so you can bet they're watching you!

750. In the Reflecting Pool in Washington, D.C.

Reflecting pools are designed to inspire solemnity and inner reflection. The reflecting pool in Washington, D.C., has been the site of many historic events. Make your own history by having sex in or near this famous landmark.

BEST POSITION Dancer or Standing Doggy Style

PROS The water is cool on a hot summer day and the scenery is incredible.

CONS While you often see movie actors standing in the pool, it may not be so easy for you. You'll have to be quick and inconspicuous.

751. At the Top of Mount Rushmore

Take a hike to the top of Mount Rushmore and have sex with the presidents.

BEST POSITION Missionary or Dancer

PROS You can enjoy the incredible view while enjoying a piece of history.

CONS It's a long trek for sex, but it'll be worth it when you get there.

752. At Hershey Park

This is a trip that chocolate lovers simply cannot miss! Take the opportunity to get naked and cover yourselves in chocolate syrup!

BEST POSITION Dancer or Standing Doggy Style

PROS You can enjoy the theme park, chocolate, and a sexy weekend.

CONS You can't actually cover yourselves in chocolate syrup while in the park—at least not while naked.

753. At the Great Smoky Mountains National Park in the Middle of Fall

There is no more beautiful place to see the colors of autumn than at Great Smoky Mountains National Park. The park also features many remote roads and trails where you can enjoy each other to the fullest.

BEST POSITION Missionary or Dancer

PROS The scenery is absolutely beautiful.

CONS This is a very remote mountain region, so don't get lost. They may not find you until the spring.

754. At the Hoover Dam

The roaring waters of the Colorado river are held at bay by the Hoover Dam. What it can't hold back is the roaring flames of passion you and your lover can make there.

BEST POSITION Dancer or Bodyguard

PROS It's incredibly passionate to make love to your partner while the water is rushing below you.

CONS It's very touristy, so you'll have to get creative to find some alone time.

755. At the Lincoln Memorial

You've heard about other people doing it; why not try having sex on the Lincoln Memorial yourself! Are you brave enough to do it right on Lincoln's lap?

BEST POSITION Mastery or Game's On

PROS If you can get away with it, you definitely have bragging rights.

CONS If not, you may get some jail time or a fine instead.

756. At the Top of the Empire State Building

You and your partner will feel like you're on top of the world when you're on top of the Empire State Building—and each other.

BEST POSITION Bodyguard or Standing Doggy Style

PROS How many people can say they've had sex while overlooking an entire city from that high in the air?

CONS It's very touristy, but there are many corners where you can hide.

757. At the Top of the Stratosphere in Las Vegas

The Stratosphere is an incredible tower in the very heart of Las Vegas. Walk around the Stratosphere to find the best dark corner that gives you privacy but still allows you to see all the sparkling city lights below.

BEST POSITION Bodyguard or Standing Doggy Style

PROS What happens in Vegas stays in Vegas.

CONS People have the tendency to go crazy in Las Vegas—sometimes this is okay and fun, sometimes not.

758. At the Wave Organ in San Francisco, CA

This beautiful sculpture is a huge organ crafted out of old cemetery ruins and is actually an organ that plays music based on how the waves crash against the bottom of the pipes.

BEST POSITION Missionary or Lotus

PROS What a romantic and really unique way to experience your partner and the beautiful sound of the ocean!

CONS It's a touristy area, so you might have a difficult time finding a private spot.

759. On a Blanket in the Middle of the Valley of Fire State Park, NV

There's something ultra-sexual about being in the middle of the desert with just you, your partner, and a blanket.

BEST POSITION Spread Eagle or Deep Stick

PROS It's hot and fiery, just like your passion!

CONS Don't get lost in the desert and don't get sand where you don't want it.

760. While Touring a Coffee Farm

Visit the Holualoa Coffee Farm on the big island of Hawaii and enjoy some good coffee and a quickie in the factory.

BEST POSITION Missionary or Cowgirl

PROS It's a great opportunity to go to Hawaii and a truly unique place to have sex.

CONS It may be challenging to get away from the tour so you'll need to get creative.

761. During a Live Event at the Fox Theater

Recently, the Fox Theater has been remodeled and it's a great place if you enjoy distinctive architecture and style. Check out the website (*www. foxdream.com*) to get a better sense of the venue and the acts playing there.

BEST POSITION Game's On or Lap Dance

PROS Enjoy some awesome music while you orgasm.

CONS It's a public venue, so be aware of your surroundings.

762. During a White House Tour

While you may not be able to run wild around the White House, you can certainly sneak into one of the bathrooms for a quickie. If a better opportunity presents itself then by all means take it!

BEST POSITION Dancer or Standing Oral

PROS A visit to the White House is something that everyone should do once in their lives. It's such a huge part of American History—so you can feel good about yourselves.

CONS The security is very tight, so it's more challenging to break away from the group.

763. At the Georgia Aquarium

Have sex at the largest aquarium in the world!

BEST POSITION Bodyguard or Standing Doggy Style

PROS It's like having sex underwater without being underwater.

CONS It's a public aquarium so watch out for little ones running around.

764. At the White Sands National Monument

The White Sands National Monument is surrounded by the White Sands Missile Range. You can have sex while missiles fly overhead—if you dare. However, the military doesn't like spectators while they're playing with missiles so you'll have to sneak in for the "missiles overhead" part.

BEST POSITION Missionary or Cowgirl

PROS It's a beautiful area with or without missiles flying by.

CONS There's a distinct possibility of getting arrested if you sneak in during missile exercises.

765. In Egypt, TX

While you're touring America, why not spend the night in Historic Egypt, Texas.

BEST POSITION Anything goes!

PROS You can shake up this quiet little town with your screams of ecstasy.

CONS You may be asked to leave shortly thereafter.

766. On Mars (or in Mars, PA)

While you can't actually have sex on Mars, you can have sex in Mars, Pennsylvania! Rent a room or just stop at a diner for a quickie. Have sex on the Mars "Flying Saucer." It's a statue that looks like a flyer saucer that sits near the small town square in the town of Mars.

BEST POSITION Anything goes!

PROS It's a small town but at least there's a spaceship.

CONS If caught having sex on the spaceship, you'll probably be escorted out of town.

767. In Amsterdam, PA

If you need a break on the three-and-a-half-hour drive from Pittsburgh, Pennsylvania, to Erie, New York, the half way point is Amsterdam, Pennsylvania. Stop in the quaint little town of Amsterdam for a sex break.

BEST POSITION Anything goes!

PROS You can say the you had a layover in Amsterdam!

CONS Unless you're on the way from Pittsburgh to Erie, there's really no other reason to stop. Unless you're from Amsterdam of course . . .

768. In New York's Little Italy

Forget a slice of pizza. Experience the Italian flavor of New York by sneaking off to somewhere in Little Italy and getting it on. Mamma mia!

BEST POSITION Dancer or Standing Oral

PROS Really good sex can make you start speaking Italian—or at least in tongues.

CONS Dark alleys in New York can be dangerous places to be!

769. At the Smithsonian

You can't tour America and not visit the Smithsonian—or Washington, D.C., for that matter! Both are American icons.

BEST POSITION Dancer or Bodyguard

PROS There are plenty of dark corners and empty hallways for a quickie.

CONS It's a public place so watch your surroundings.

770. In Pele's Bath, HI

This incredible ocean pool is separated from the big waves by a simple, man-made sea wall. It is also naturally heated to about ninety degrees by the volcanic magma underneath—it's like bathing in a tropical paradise!

BEST POSITION Dancer or Bodyguard

PROS This one sounds better than a boring hot spring.

CONS You will need to travel to Hawaii—and that's kind of far and expensive.

771. At Frederick's of Hollywood in Hollywood, CA

Frederick's of Hollywood is synonymous with glamorous ladies' undergarments. Stop into their museum to see how lingerie has evolved over the past fifty years. Go into the dressing room together to try on lingerie. That will give you some ideas.

BEST POSITION Game's On or Standing Doggy Style

PROS You might end up with some really sexy lingerie.

CONS You may get kicked out of the store.

772. In the Crayola Crayon Factory

Visit the factory in Easton, Pennsylvania—and then express your sexual creativity back at the hotel. Try your hand at body painting.

BEST POSITION Dancer or Standing Oral

PROS Crayons have been around for more than 100 years and have shaped childhood visions and artistic inspirations for millions of children.

CONS There are a lot of children around, so be careful not to get caught! It's probably better to carry your sexual creativity back to the hotel.

773. In the Dragon Cave of Casa Bonita

Casa Bonita is an incredible restaurant in the heart of Denver, Colorado. There are flame throwers, divers, and incredible Mexican food. Check out the dragon cave first and find out what treasures lie within.

BEST POSITION Dancer or Bodyguard

PROS Have a great dinner, enjoy a wonderful show and have sex in a cave. It doesn't get much better than that!

CONS Little ones love to wander in the cave as well. So make sure you can't be seen easily, although you'll probably be able to hear people if they approach.

774. At Niagara Falls, NY, after Dark

Enjoy the view of Niagara Falls at night while enjoying your partner at the same time. The view of the falls is particularly beautiful at night when the falls are lit up by different colors of lighting.

BEST POSITION Doggy Style or Cradle

PROS It's simply beautiful and awe inspiring . . .

CONS It's a very family friendly environment, so watch out for the kiddos.

775. In the Hugh Hefner Sky Villa at the Palms Hotel in Las Vegas

If you are lucky enough to stay in the Hugh Hefner Sky Villa and you don't get totally kinky freaky, there's something wrong with you!

BEST POSITION Anything goes!

PROS This is a fantasy suite designed for absolute luxury.

CONS It costs about $40,000 per night. The good news is that it will hold 250 people, so that's only $160 per night per person if you can get 248 people to go with you.

776. In the Middle of Central Park

A lot of things happen in Central Park, and if you and your partner catch a quickie behind a bush, you won't be the first ones to have done so.

BEST POSITION Missionary or Doggy Style

PROS It's amazing how this beautiful park exists in such total harmony with this sprawling metropolis. You have to see it to believe it.

CONS You might meet some strange people—a can of pepper spray on your keychain is never a bad idea.

777. In the Middle of New Orleans During Mardi Gras

Mardi Gras in New Orleans is the craziest party in America. If you want to have sex in the middle of huge crowd of people, this is the place.

BEST POSITION Standing Doggy Style or Dancer

PROS The wilder you get the more beads you get.

CONS New Orleans is not exactly a clean city, especially during Mardi Gras, so keep this in mind!

778. In the Middle of Times Square on New Year's as the Ball Is Dropping

Celebrate the New Year with a mind blowing orgasm. There are so many people, that you won't even be noticed and if you are, who cares?

BEST POSITION Dancer or Bodyguard

PROS There's no better way to ring in the New Year.

CONS There are A LOT of people—this could scare some of you.

779. At Fisherman's Wharf in San Francisco

Fisherman's Wharf in San Francisco, California, offers history, culture, and food. Make a weekend of it, enjoy the sights and see how many different places you can have sex with your partner—outside of your hotel room.

BEST POSITION Standing Doggy Style or Bodyguard

PROS San Francisco is a great weekend getaway.

CONS There's so much too see, be careful not to wear yourself out—remember, you're here for a sexual rendezvous. The history and culture can come later.

780. In the Trump Tower

How can you visit Manhattan without going to the Trump World Tower for a quickie? It's a must see on your tour of America checklist.

BEST POSITION Dancer or Standing Doggy Style

PROS It's a huge building so you'll have fun finding a secluded place for a quickie. They even have residential units if you want to pretend to be a prospective buyer.

CONS The residences start around $1,000,000—so you better look the part.

781. In the Yellowstone Thermal Areas

Get back to nature with a romp in the wild. There are a number of thermal areas in Yellowstone National Park, which are a bit different from hot springs. Find a place where cold water meets hot and you've got an incredible nature-made bath.

BEST POSITION Dancer or Standing Doggy Style

PROS Nature's incredible thermal areas are perfect for warm bathing and making passionate love—or having steamy, raunchy sex! It's up to you!

CONS Make sure you don't end up taking a dip in water that is too hot.

782. Inside Sam Hill's Stonehenge

Have sex inside Sam Hill's Stonehenge in Maryhill, Washington. This almost identical copy of the more famous English Stonehenge was built as a memorial to those who died in World War I. This is one roadside site that you won't want to miss.

BEST POSITION Missionary or Lotus

PROS You don't have to travel all the way to Ireland to see Stonehenge!

CONS It's not the real prehistoric Stonehenge.

783. Inside the Statue of Liberty

Doesn't the Statue of Liberty represent freedom? It's time to feel free by experiencing your partner in the statue that truly makes America the "Land of the Free."

BEST POSITION Dancer or Bodyguard

PROS It's a great way to celebrate your freedom.

CONS It's pretty cramped inside the actual statue so you may have to settle for the visitor area beneath the statue.

784. On Rodeo Drive in Beverly Hills, CA

Spend the day shopping, star watching, and getting freaky with your partner.

BEST POSITION Bodyguard or Standing Oral

PROS You'll likely see a movie star or two.

CONS Unless you find a really good sale, shopping on Rodeo Drive can get very expensive.

785. On Top of the Serpent Mound in OH

According to Wikipedia, the Great Serpent Mound is a 1,330-foot-long, three-foot-high prehistoric effigy mound located on a plateau of the Serpent Mound crater along Brush Creek in Adams County, Ohio. It's believed to have been built around A.D. 1050 for ceremonial and calendrical purposes.

BEST POSITION Standing Doggy Style or Mastery

PROS It's a great place to have a roll in the grass.

CONS It's pretty open so try to find a more secluded area.

786. On Top of the World's Largest Laptop

Check out the World's Largest Laptop at Time Warner Center in New York. You can actually type with your feet. What other body parts come to mind?

BEST POSITION Doggy Style or Bodyguard

PROS You can type an interesting message.

CONS It's doubtful that you'll actually be able to have sex on the laptop unless you're extremely resourceful.

787. At Johnson's Shut-Ins State Park in MO

Have some sexy fun on the natural water slides formed by rocks in the river or while you're hiking through the park.

BEST POSITION Missionary or Game's On

PROS It's a really cool area to play in the water and with each other.

CONS The area is still recovering from a huge flood caused by the failure of a dam upriver, but is scheduled to reopen in 2009.

788. Polar Bear Bed in the Aurora Ice Museum at the Chena Hot Springs Resort in AK

The Aurora Ice Museum is the world's only year-round ice environment. It features amazing ice sculptures and even an ice bar that serves appletinis in carved ice martini glasses. Sneak away to the polar bear bedroom and have sex on a real polar bear rug.

BEST POSITION Missionary or Spoons

PROS The appletinis in carved ice martini glasses.

CONS The entire place is made of ice—Brr . . .

789. The Roanoke Star

The neon star at the top of Mill Mountain in Roanoke, VA, is an incredible observation deck allows you to overlook the entire city as it's lit up at night. This is a great place to visit with a lover.

BEST POSITION Bodyguard or Standing Doggy Style

PROS It's romantic, raunchy, and sexy!

CONS It's not likely you'll get caught because it's very private. You should, however, be watchful of bugs.

790. Tour of the Coors Beer Factory in Golden, CO

What man doesn't like the combination of beer and sex? Make the most of it and get a little freaky on a beer tour.

BEST POSITION Dancer or Standing Doggy Style

PROS Sex and beer—do you really need anything else?

CONS Factories can be dangerous places because of all of the equipment required to manufacture mass quantities of beer. You wouldn't want to be buried in a gigantic vat of hops!

791. Trolley in San Francisco

If you've never been to San Francisco, you can make a great first impression!

BEST POSITION Standing Doggy Style or Bodyguard

PROS On a trolley, you can do it standing or sitting.

CONS It's very public and very easy to get caught and kicked off the trolley.

792. Under a Quilt During an Amish Buggy Ride

Visit Arthur, Illinois, during the annual Amish Quilt Festival. Enjoy a sexual buggy ride snuggled under a real Amish Quilt.

BEST POSITION Game's On or Mastery

PROS You can get away with lots of things under a quilt.

CONS But you probably won't be able to get away with getting totally naked.

793. Under the Grapes in Sonoma Valley

Enjoy a sexual romp in Sonoma Valley on a tour of the wine country.

BEST POSITION Missionary or Cowgirl

PROS Enjoy some good wine and great sex.

CONS Be watchful of all the grapes on the ground lest you come back with stains all over your back.

794. Underneath the Hollywood Sign

You'll feel rich, famous, and scandalous just like the celebrities do!

BEST POSITION Dancer or Standing Doggy Style

PROS If you can get close enough to the sign without getting caught, it's an incredible thrill!

CONS It's illegal to go near the sign, and there are plenty of cameras and security guards too.

CHAPTER 20

THE MOST SACRILEGIOUS PLACES TO HAVE SEX

This section will seem sacrilegious to some, and it will seem fun and exciting to others. Either way, you can enjoy broadening your horizons and try some of these out yourself, if you're brave enough to be seen in the eyes of you-know-who.

795. In a Cemetery under a Full Moon

If you like Halloween adventures, dress up in the proper costumes, go to a cemetery, and have sex over one of the headstones or lying down on one of the graves.

BEST POSITION Delight or Standing Doggy Style over a head stone

PROS It's different and definitely kinky.

CONS You may not be the only one planning something unusual in the cemetery that night, so keep your eyes open.

796. In the Back of a Hearse

Continuing with the death theme—why not have sex in the back of a hearse? Just think of all of the dead bodies and spirits that have been in there (or still might be). If that doesn't give you goose bumps, maybe your partner will?

BEST POSITION Missionary or 69

PROS It's still kinky, but not as taboo as a cemetery.

CONS It might be hard to find a hearse.

797. In a Display Casket at the Store

Take it to the next level and have sex in a casket. You can do this by going casket shopping. Tell them you want to lie in it to test the size and then ask for privacy because, after all, this is a very personal matter to you.

BEST POSITION Missionary or 69

PROS The casket is very cozy and intimate.

CONS Space can be very tight and you may not be able to get the salesperson to leave you alone with the casket.

798. In a Funeral Home Viewing Room

Most of us go to funeral homes to mourn, but bring your mood up by getting it on in the viewing room.

BEST POSITION Game's On or 69

PROS This is a great way to push each others' boundaries (and everyone else's, for that matter, if you get caught!).

CONS There are rumors that some of these retailers actually reuse caskets. You may not be the first to lie down in the casket.

799. Pet Cemetery

This is an interesting twist on the cemetery idea. It's questionable whether this is more or less creepy than the human cemetery—only you and your partner can decide this for yourselves.

BEST POSITION Dancer or Standing Doggy Style

PROS It's a great opportunity get over those old fears from watching too many Stephen King movies as a kid.

CONS If you get caught, it's doubtful the other person will understand what you're doing or why.

800. In a Monastery

While normally reserved for prayer and contemplation, create your own religious experience in a monastery, with your lover.

BEST POSITION Missionary or Cowgirl

PROS The energy is very peaceful in a monastery.

CONS The peaceful energy may be disturbed if you're caught having sex.

801. In a Mosque

You might have to travel a bit further to find a mosque, but depending on your beliefs it might be worth the trip. Just be careful about where you go; a couple was actually sentenced to jail time for having sex in a mosque, in Africa. The judge said, "Having sex in a mosque is a most abominable thing to religion." Check out the article and avoid this mosque at: *http://atheism.about.com/b/2006/10/22/couple-sentenced-for-having-sex-in-mosque.htm.*

BEST POSITION Missionary or Dancer

PROS If you get away with it, you'll get a rush of excitement.

CONS If you don't, you might get jail time.

802. In a Synagogue

Jewish or not, if you're going to desecrate one religious institution, why not hit all of the big ones?

BEST POSITION Missionary or Dancer

PROS You can enjoy your own version of spirituality with each other.

CONS Even though it may seem okay to you, it may not be okay to the people who choose to worship there.

803. In a Buddhist Temple

Surely the Buddhists will be more accepting of sex?

BEST POSITION Missionary or Lotus

PROS Buddhist temples are incredibly peaceful and spiritual places which may allow you to take your sexual experience to new heights.

CONS According to Buddhism, seeking "things" that we think will bring us pleasure in actuality creates much of our pain. So the physical attachment to sex can actually be a bad thing.

804. At a Wiccan Ritual

Some, not all, Wiccan groups actually use Sex Magick in their rituals. When done in the proper context this can be a very powerful sexual experience. The term Sex Magick can be something as simple as setting an intention for your sexual experience. It's not all about evil power and raising the dead. Most Wiccan groups consist of peaceful and loving people. You do not have to be Wiccan to practice Sex Magick.

BEST POSITION Missionary or Cowgirl

PROS Wiccans are far more accepting of others and of individual sexuality.

CONS Just like other religions, there are differences in beliefs among subgroups. Talk with the people you're hanging out with to understand their individual beliefs.

805. At a Séance

Get freaky with the dead. It doesn't get much cooler or scarier than this!

BEST POSITION Anything goes!

PROS You never know what's going to happen.

CONS You never know what's going to happen.

806. At a Satanic Ritual on Halloween

Partake in some exploratory satanic rituals on the Day of the Dead and see what happens! This doesn't have to be a real satanic ritual, just make it a really fun Halloween party for two or more.

BEST POSITION Missionary or Doggy Style

PROS It's a great opportunity to dress up in full costume and enjoy a really sexy Halloween party.

CONS Be careful not to accidentally perform a real satanic ritual. There's no telling what you may conjure up!

807. In a Church Parking Lot

Get in your car for a quickie either before or after the church service.

BEST POSITION Cowgirl or Deck Chair

PROS If your windows are tinted, no one will notice. Just remember to fix your clothes before you get out.

CONS Your Sunday Best may get a little wrinkled.

808. In the Bell Tower of Your Church

Celebrate each other by ringing each others' bells.

BEST POSITION Dancer or Bodyguard

PROS You can feel the vibration when the bells "gong."

CONS Your ears might be ringing for days.

809. In Front of the Altar at Church

Kneel down for a prayer and a blessing—from your partner!

BEST POSITION Missionary or Standing Doggy Style

PROS You're kneeling, the rest will come naturally.

CONS You may be struck by lightning.

810. Leaning on the Pulpit

Get some action while giving a sermon. Depending on the pulpit, you may be able to hide under there for a surprise visit.

BEST POSITION Standing Oral or Manual Stimulation

PROS This is a fun way to surprise your partner.

CONS He or she may not be able to keep a straight face—especially in front of the entire congregation!

811. In the Choir

You can lie down or sit in the seats of the choir pews for some sexy fun. Try this after hours or the priest might silence your song before you're done.

BEST POSITION Missionary or Standing Doggy Style

PROS Churches are often open at all hours of the day and night to welcome their parishioners to pray whenever they need it.

CONS If you get caught, you'll be at confession for months.

812. In the Baptismal Pool

Some might say it's sacrilegious, but depending on your moral or religious beliefs, a frisky dip in a baptismal could be fun.

BEST POSITION Dancer or Standing Doggy Style

PROS It's dirty and fun all at the same time. What better way to cool off after a stuffy church service?

CONS Why do you think the babies cry so much when the water touches their heads? The water is freezing!

813. On a Church Pew

You can enjoy each other in the back row of the pews during a boring service or go all out and lie down for some missionary action once everyone else has left.

BEST POSITION Missionary or Manual Stimulation

PROS If it all goes well, you'll get some blessings from your partner.

CONS Most church pews are not padded so they're uncomfortable—they're supposed to keep you awake.

814. Under a Church Pew

Whether you're religious or not, there's something sexy and definitely forbidden about having sex underneath a church pew.

BEST POSITION Missionary or Spoons

PROS It's forbidden, it's lusty—what's not to love?

CONS Even though you're a bit more hidden than if you were on top of the pew, you might get caught. Watch out for church cleaners and old ladies who forget their umbrellas!

815. In the Confessional

Feeling guilty about having sex under the pew? Step into the confessional for a quickie so that you can sin and be forgiven at the same time.

BEST POSITION Lap Dance or Mastery

PROS You can sin and confess in the same place.

CONS It may actually be considered a sin (or at least highly inappropriate) to have sex in a confessional.

CHAPTER 21

TRULY REDNECK PLACES

The intent here is not to offend—but let's face it; some of us are more in tune with our country roots than others. Here are some fun places to help us reconnect with our inner redneck.

816. At the County Fair

Get back to your country roots at the county fair. If you grew up in the city, experience a different way of life all together. Either way, you'll have a great time rolling in the hay with your lover.

BEST POSITION Missionary or Cowgirl

PROS There will be lots of places to grab a quickie.

CONS The smell of animals, and everything seems to move at half speed.

817. Next to Big Tex at the Texas State Fair

The Texas State Fair is held every October in Dallas. Big Tex is a giant fifty-two-foot statue that welcomes guests to the state fair. Get your picture taken with Big Tex—naked!

BEST POSITION Dancer or Bodyguard

PROS Who else has a picture next to Big Tex naked?

CONS Big Tex is at the main entry to the State Fair of Texas so you may not make it into the fair.

818. In the Car Lift at an Auto Shop

This is easier if you or your partner work at an auto shop, but you might be able to get away with it even if you don't! In the car, of course. Just don't rock the car too much!

BEST POSITION Mastery or Deck Chair

PROS Turn an ordinary trip to the auto shop into something incredibly fun and memorable.

CONS It can be a little dangerous. There's always the chance the lift will malfunction and fall—but it's slim.

819. On a Hunting Platform in a Tree

If you or your partner likes to hunt, a hunting platform in a tree might be the perfect place for an early morning romp while you wait for the deer to arrive.

BEST POSITION Lotus or Cradle

PROS It's a good excuse to get up early.

CONS You may miss the deer.

820. At the Local Gun Show

If you or your partner likes guns, then you'll likely find yourselves at the local gun show every year. Why not create some sparks of your own while you're there?

BEST POSITION Dancer or Bodyguard

PROS You're going to be there anyway.

CONS Do not play with loaded guns.

821. Against an Old-Fashioned Windmill

You know the type of windmills that farmers still use today to pump water to their livestock watering tanks? You can even splash in the tank if it's warm.

BEST POSITION Dancer or Standing Doggy Style

PROS You'll be out in the country so it's unlikely that you'll get caught.

CONS Old-fashioned windmills are often made of wood so watch out for splinters and ants.

822. In a Horse Stall of a Barn

Take a roll in the hay, just stay out of the horses apples—and remember not to walk behind them and scare them unless you want to get kicked.

BEST POSITION Cowgirl or Doggy Style

PROS It's dirty, romantic, and incredibly fun all at the same time.

CONS You might want to bring a blanket, because hay doesn't feel that great against naked skin!

823. In the Middle of a Cow Pasture

Country folk won't mind getting frisky in a cow pasture—after all, what better way to take a break from a hard day's work?

BEST POSITION Cowgirl or Standing Doggy Style

PROS What's better than a quickie in the middle of nowhere?

CONS Cow paddies.

824. Next to the Scarecrow in the Field

It's not Big Tex, but if you don't live in Texas, it'll have to do!

BEST POSITION Dancer or Bodyguard

PROS The good news is that you can get away with *much* more in the middle of the field next to a scarecrow than you can next to Big Tex.

CONS Scarecrows are normally filled with hay, which is very poky on your skin—try to avoid using the scarecrow as a prop in any of your positions.

825. On the Fence Around Your Farm

Try doing something different and making love to your partner while perched on the fence surrounding your property.

BEST POSITION Spread Eagle or Standing Doggy Style

PROS There's something fun and frisky about being naked in the middle of a farm.

CONS Don't try it on an electric cattle fence!

826. In the Loft of a Barn Full of Hay

Climb up to the loft and enjoy a roll in the hay.

BEST POSITION Missionary or Cowgirl

PROS It's private and cozy.

CONS Hay is very poky—bring a blanket.

827. In a Monster Truck

Hop in the cab for some really redneck sex.

BEST POSITION Mastery or Deck Chair

PROS It's just like a car, only bigger.

CONS You'll need a ladder to get up there.

828. In the Back of a Monster Truck

When you're finished in the cab, head on back to the truck bed. You can add some romance by making a soft bed in the back.

BEST POSITION Mastery or Standing Doggy Style

PROS You get a great view because you're up so high.

CONS Don't roll out. It's a long way down.

829. In a Monster Truck Tire

This is the easiest way to have sex in a monster truck—just climb into the tire.

BEST POSITION Mastery or Standing Doggy Style

PROS You can't do this on a normal truck!

CONS Make sure the truck has been washed first and that no one will drive off while you're standing in the tire.

830. Under the Bleachers at a Monster Truck Rally

Don't have a hookup on a monster truck? Then you'll have to settle for sex under the bleachers at the rally.

BEST POSITION Dancer or Standing Oral

PROS You don't have to worry about anyone driving off while you're in the middle of a hot sexcapade.

CONS It's not exactly the Four Seasons.

831. At a Public Laundromat

There's something deliciously raunchy about bending over a running washer and letting your partner take you. Bring a public element to it by doing it at a Laundromat!

BEST POSITION Spread Eagle or Standing Doggy Style

PROS Having sex on a washer is fun. Having sex on a washer in a public Laundromat is kinky and incredibly exhilarating.

CONS You stand a good chance of getting caught or seen by someone. Go late at night to reduce the risk.

832. In the Sleeper of a Semi Truck

Sleepers in these big trucks can be quite plush, albeit small. Cuddle up for some kinky sex at the truck stop!

BEST POSITION Missionary or Spoons

PROS It's just like a miniature bedroom, so let your imagination run wild.

CONS There's not a lot of space so you can't get too crazy.

833. In the Back of a Moving Semi Truck Trailer

Enjoy sex on the move in the back of a semi. Make sure to hold on because the ride can be a little rough.

BEST POSITION Dancer or Standing Doggy Style

PROS It's a relatively safe way to have sex while going down the highway, and you'll be safe from prying eyes.

CONS It's still dangerous to have sex in a moving vehicle.

834. In the Cab of an Eighteen-Wheel Truck

Make use of the roomy cab in these trucks to enjoy a big ride in a big rig.

BEST POSITION Game's On or Mastery

PROS Lots of room to try different positions.

CONS Watch out for the air horn or you may draw unwanted attention.

835. On the Sofa at a Truck Stop Lounge

Grab a quickie on the sofa the next time you stop in for "all you can eat."

BEST POSITION Mastery or Game's On

PROS It's a laid back place to get your freak on.

CONS You may end up with an audience.

836. At One of Those "Sleep Only" Motels

Spend the night at a "sleep only" motel and use the public showers in the morning. It will help you remember to be thankful for life's little luxuries.

BEST POSITION Anything goes!

PROS Get kinky freaky all night long.

CONS You're going to want a shower sooner rather than later.

837. In a Tool or Storage Shed

Sneak into the tool shed out back for a quickie.

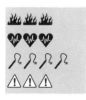

BEST POSITION Dancer or Bodyguard

PROS No one will look for you in there.

CONS It's dirty and musty.

838. In a Truck Stop Shower

It is a public shower so enjoy some public sex in the shower.

BEST POSITION Standing Doggy Style or Standing Oral

PROS You will not likely be interrupted.

CONS It may not be the cleanest shower so be aware of where you put various body parts.

839. In a Wheelbarrow

Nothing says Daisy Duke like riding around in a wheelbarrow wearing your shortest shorts.

BEST POSITION Cradle or Standing Doggy Style

PROS It can be fun to ride around in a wheelbarrow.

CONS You may be limited to leaning over the wheelbarrow for actual intercourse.

840. In a Farmer's Field

Lie down on a blanket for a picnic lunch and something sexy for dessert.

BEST POSITION Missionary or Deck Chair

PROS It's very romantic and peaceful.

CONS The farmer may not be so peaceful if he catches you in his field.

841. At a Cheap Roadside Diner

Try to find one of those diners that looks like a train car.

BEST POSITION Game's On or Dancer

PROS It's very nostalgic and reminiscent of the 1950s.

CONS You may be relegated to the bathroom once again, but you can play under the table as foreplay.

842. At the Dollar Store

A quick trip to the dollar store definitely calls for a cheap quickie! Take an trip to the dollar store and jazz it up, so you'll look forward to it next time!

BEST POSITION Game's On or Dancer

PROS You'll definitely get your money's worth!

CONS Dollar stores can be very busy, so go during off-peak hours.

843. At Your Local Farmer's Market

Enjoy squeezing her melons. Crawl under a display table for privacy.

BEST POSITION Missionary or Spoons

PROS You'll have fresh fruit and veggies to snack on when you're done.

CONS It's going to be dirty under the table, so make sure to dust your clothes off when you climb out.

844. On a Four-Wheeler in the Middle of the Country

Take a dirt trail adventure with your lover to a private and secluded spot. Take advantage of the ability to get to places no one else can.

BEST POSITION Mastery or Lap Dance

PROS It's a fun and new way to experience the great outdoors.

CONS Having sex on a moving four-wheeler can be dangerous.

845. While Riding in a Go-Kart

Bring back the nostalgia of riding go-karts when you were a kid in a very adult way. Sitting is pretty much the only position you're going to be able to work with in a go-kart and even it is a little questionable. It just depends on the size and layout of the go-kart.

BEST POSITION Mastery or Lap Dance

PROS It makes a trip around the go-kart track a heck of a lot more fun!

CONS You risk getting seen by children and worse— parents of children!

846. In the Back of a Ford Pickup

Create a soft pallet in the bed of your pickup truck on hot summer night. Spend the whole night together looking at the stars and fulfilling your fantasies.

BEST POSITION Missionary or Cowgirl

PROS It's like camping without a tent.

CONS Mosquitoes and other things that go buzz in the night.

847. In the Chicken Coop

Hide from the kids or even your parents by sneaking off to the chicken coop for a quickie on a weekend afternoon.

BEST POSITION Standing Doggy Style or Dancer

PROS What a raunchy way to have fun on the farm!

CONS Chicken poop—need we say more?

848. On the Midway at the State Fair

Get back to your country roots by taking a trip to the State Fair and while you're there, enjoy some roasted corn, a funnel cake, and a quickie on the midway. If you've never been to a fair before, the midway is spot where the fun, food, and games booths can be found.

BEST POSITION Dancer or Bodyguard

PROS Funnel cake and giant corn on the cob—the pros are once you come out of the porta-potty.

CONS Eeewwww!

849. In a Livestock Stall at the State Fair

Find a clean stall—this might be your biggest challenge—and enjoy a 'roll in the hay' with your partner.

BEST POSITION Missionary or Standing Doggy Style

PROS If you go in the evening, you should be mostly undisturbed.

CONS The smell of farm animals.

850. In the Restroom of a Moving Greyhound Bus

This is the redneck version of the mile-high club.

BEST POSITION Dancer or Bodyguard

PROS It's a great place for a quickie.

CONS Just downright icky! Watch what you touch.

851. In the Waiting Room of an Auto Shop

Waiting for your car to be done can be very boring, so why not add a little excitement by getting frisky in the waiting room of the auto shop?

BEST POSITION Dancer or Standing Doggy Style

PROS Instead of passing the time reading magazines, you're taking time to enjoy your partner instead.

CONS You can definitely get caught; especially if you try this at a place with an all-glass waiting area.

852. In the Service Bay at the Auto Shop

Climb down into the service bay for some greasy, sexy fun.

BEST POSITION Missionary or Standing Doggy Style

PROS You'll be out of sight from the customers.

CONS It's very dirty and greasy, so wear some old clothes or none at all.

853. On a Mechanical Bull

While it might be tough to stay on the mechanical bull, it's worth a shot!

BEST POSITION Mastery or Lap Dance

PROS There's a very high orgasm potential if done right.

CONS You may get injured if you fall off the bull.

854. In an Abandoned Barn Wearing Nothing but Boots and a Cowboy Hat

This is another great photo opportunity because old barns are so beautiful and rustic. It makes for a great backdrop for some sexy pictures—and for a fun romp once you finish clicking those photos!

BEST POSITION Cowgirl or Dancer

PROS You'll definitely have privacy.

CONS Make sure the place is stable and doesn't fall in on you.

855. On Top of a Hay Bale in the Middle of a Field

Go for an old-fashioned roll in the hay. You'll love the view from up on top of the hay bale—and the view of your partner.

BEST POSITION Dancer or Standing Doggy Style

PROS There's nothing that's quite as country, and as sexy, as getting a little dirty on top of a hay bale.

CONS Bring a blanket—hay can irritate nude skin.

856. In the Cab of a Giant Tractor

Many men have played with replicas of gigantic tractors when they were kids—so fulfill the fantasy they didn't know they had and get busy in the cab!

BEST POSITION Mastery or Lap Dance

PROS It can make plowing the field more entertaining.

CONS Don't lose sight of the field or you might have to have some neighbor's crops replanted.

857. Riding the Lawnmower in Your Backyard

Take a break from working hard on the lawn and treat yourself to a little top-of-the-mower sex play! If you're coordinated enough, you can even get randy while driving it!

BEST POSITION Mastery or Lap Dance

PROS It takes the work right out of the chore of mowing the lawn!

CONS Be careful not to fall off the riding lawnmower, and if you do, get out of the way quickly!

858. On a Tire Swing at an Old Barn

You can build a tire swing using just a strong rope and an old tire!

BEST POSITION Standing Doggy Style or Cradle

PROS Use the swing's momentum to aid your thrusting!

CONS Be careful of sharp points and rubber burns.

CHAPTER 22

BEST PLACES
FOR SPORTS
ENTHUSIASTS

The title says it all. If you consider yourself an athlete or just a sports supporter, then you'll want to check out the following places.

859. In the Luxury Box at Any Sporting Event

You can have sex and watch the game—just make sure to lock the door.

BEST POSITION Anything goes!

PROS There's no better way to attend a sporting event.

CONS It could be expensive unless you get a corporate hookup.

860. In an Empty Stadium on the Fifty-Yard Line

Celebrate victory by having sex on the fifty-yard line after the football game.

BEST POSITION Missionary or Cowgirl

PROS It's an incredible way to celebrate.

CONS Watch out for stadium security.

861. At Your Team's Stadium

Whether it's the New York Giants or Notre Dame, visit your team's stadium and explore the venue for places to get your game on.

BEST POSITION Dancer or Standing Doggy Style

PROS When someone asks what you did this weekend, you'll have a great answer.

CONS The stadium will be packed, so finding a good spot may take some patience and creativity.

862. At the Super Bowl

This is the ultimate for football fans. Even better if you score a luxury box!

BEST POSITION Anything goes!

PROS Sex in a luxury box is good. Sex in a luxury box at the Super Bowl is awesome!

CONS Good luck getting a luxury box at the Super Bowl.

863. During an NBA Playoff Game

This is the ultimate for basketball fans. It'll be even better if you can score a luxury box!

BEST POSITION Anything goes!

PROS Sex in a luxury box is good. Sex in a luxury box at the NBA Playoffs is awesome!

CONS While a little easier to get than a luxury box at the Super Bowl, it's still a premium item.

864. At a Basketball Game During March Madness

Another option, if you're more of a college hoops fan, is to 'score' at a game during March Madness, the NCAA Basketball tournament.

BEST POSITION Dancer or Bodyguard

PROS The emotion is higher at the college playoffs— they still have a lot to gain and little to lose. For these guys, it's now or never!

CONS Smaller stadiums and no luxury boxes mean that you'll have to have your fun out in the open.

865. During the Final Game of the World Series

Baseball fans, this is your day—especially if your team made it to this point. Even if you get seats behind the pole, you'll still be able to enjoy the game!

BEST POSITION Lap Dance or Standing Doggy Style

PROS You can bring a whole new meaning to the seventh inning stretch.

CONS It's very public, so you'll risk getting kicked out and missing the rest of the game.

866. At Night in the Middle of the Soccer Field

The grass is so nice on a soccer field. Use it to your advantage and enjoy a frisky romp at midfield. Then you can lie there and look at the stars.

BEST POSITION Missionary or Deck Chair

PROS Enjoy the soft grass and the stars.

CONS Once again, watch out for stadium security.

867. On Home Plate after the Big Game

If you play in a local baseball league, celebrate your home run by having sex over home plate.

BEST POSITION Standing Doggy Style or Bodyguard

PROS A new twist on "hitting a home run."

CONS Baseball dirt is very sticky if you're sweaty.

868. At the Baseball Stadium in the Top Row

Head up to the nosebleed section for a quickie during the game.

BEST POSITION Mastery or Lap Dance

PROS Unless the team is having a really good season, you'll be alone up there.

CONS Watch out for cameras or you'll end up on the big screen!

869. Basketball Court Top Row

Basketball courts are much more tightly packed and the seats and rows are very close together, so you'll have opt for her sitting in his lap—remember to dress for the occasion. You can have sex just about anywhere if you wear a loose-fitting, longer skirt.

BEST POSITION Mastery or Lap Dance

PROS You can enjoy bouncing his balls.

CONS It's very public and crowded unless you have a losing team.

870. In the Bathroom at Your Favorite Sporting Event

The bathroom is always the fall-back location if you can't make it happen anywhere else.

BEST POSITION Dancer or Standing Doggy Style

PROS It's reliable and always available.

CONS You'll miss part of the game!

871. In the Elevator at Your Favorite Sporting Event

Most of the elevators at sports venues are really slow moving, so you'll at least have time for some oral or manual action.

BEST POSITION Dancer or Manual Stimulation

PROS The elevators are rarely used.

CONS Someone may join you on the next level—just tell them that his shirt was stuck in his pants.

872. Center Court after the Big Game

He shoots, he scores . . . Learn how to really dribble your balls with a late night game of your own on the basketball court.

BEST POSITION Missionary or Deck Chair

PROS The acoustics in a basketball stadium are really cool when it's empty.

CONS And once again, watch out for stadium security.

873. In a Boxing Ring

Take off your clothes and put on your gloves for ten rounds of naked "boxing."

BEST POSITION Cowgirl or Doggy Style

PROS You can even throw in some wrestling moves to make it more interesting.

CONS It's really challenging to grab onto each other wearing boxing gloves.

874. Under the Goal Posts of a Pro Football Stadium

"He could go all the way!" Yes! Score! Having sex in the end zone or against the goal post brings back the excitement of long runs and last minute scores. Enjoy the adrenaline of the game—together.

BEST POSITION Dancer or Standing Doggy Style

PROS The goal post gives you something to hold onto for standing poses.

CONS Watch out for stadium security.

875. On Every Green of the Local Country Club

Plan to do something sexy on every single green—as foreplay—and then, on the eighteenth hole, you can have the grand finale!

BEST POSITION Try a different position for each green.

PROS Golf greens are almost as soft as a sleeping bag.

CONS Be careful not to get too tired before the eighteenth hole.

876. Celebrate a Big Win at Center Ice

After the big game, meet your significant other at center ice to celebrate.

BEST POSITION Missionary or Deck Chair

PROS The ice just seems to have a glow about it, even when the lights are off.

CONS It's ice, so bring a blanket to lie on.

877. Under a Ramp at the Skating Complex

While in-line skating, crawl under one of the ramps for a sex break.

BEST POSITION Missionary or Spoons

PROS No will notice—they're focused on not wiping out!

CONS You'll be having sex on hard, dirty concrete.

878. On a Mountain on a Beautiful Ledge

Make camp on a ledge and enjoy your lover and the view all night long.

BEST POSITION Missionary or Lotus

PROS The absolute silence and privacy when you're high up on the mountain can't be beat.

CONS Make sure that you pick a large enough ledge that you can relax and feel comfortable.

879. While Running a 10K

Celebrate finishing the race with a quickie—that's all you'll have the energy for!

BEST POSITION Missionary or Cowgirl

PROS You can share that runner's high together.

CONS Only do it if you feel up to it.

880. On a Tennis Court at Night

If you're going for a late-night romp on the tennis court, make sure you don't get your balls caught in the net!

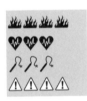

BEST POSITION Missionary or Cowgirl

PROS You'll have the opportunity to serve up something extra special to your sweetie!

CONS Opt for standing poses because tennis courts are hard, rough, and if they're clay it will get stuck to you.

881. On the Track Field

Play with the starting blocks and the hurdles. No fast starts, please!

BEST POSITION Doggy Style or Standing Oral

PROS The equipment on the track field can add some interesting positions to your repertoire.

CONS It's a public field, so stay out of sight.

882. On the Wrestling Mat

The wrestling mat is somewhat padded so you can roll around.

BEST POSITION Deck Chair or Deep Stick

PROS It's padded so feel free to get a little rough!

CONS Don't use baby oil—it'll ruin the mat.

CHAPTER 23

PLACES HARD TO FIND, BUT WORTH THE TRY!

There's creative and then there's totally unique. This section contains places that you can't find just anywhere—but if you look for them, you'll probably be happy that you did! Talk about bragging rights, it's likely that you and your partner will be the first among your group of friends to try these unique spots. Have fun!

883. At a Sex Museum

Sex museums are the perfect place to explore each other in public! You can not only learn things you never knew about sex and its history, but you can also learn things you never knew about your partner.

BEST POSITION Standing Oral or Standing Doggy Style

PROS There's no better way to experience sex-ed than to completely immerse yourself in it both mentally and physically!

CONS Public sex in a sex museum might be a little more tolerated than in other public places, but you could still get caught and thrown out. Is that so bad?

884. In a Two-Story Outhouse

Yes these do exist. Seriously. Check out this website: *www.roadsideamerica .com/set/outhouse.html*. There are several two-story outhouses in America where you can enjoy a stinky quickie.

BEST POSITION Standing Doggy Style or Dancer

PROS It's totally unique and different.

CONS The smell, obviously.

885. Next to "Christ of the Ozarks" in Eureka Springs, AK

Next to the one in Rio, they claim that this Jesus is the tallest un-crucified Christ in the world!

BEST POSITION Missionary or Lotus

PROS Once again, it's totally unique and different.

CONS Religious extremists may feel that it's blasphemous.

886. In a Clock Tower

Venture onto any college campus or center of town to find your local clock tower—and make each other go "Gong." Make sure you're there when the clock strikes noon or midnight, the vibrations are incredible!

BEST POSITION Dancer or Standing Doggy Style

PROS Intense sound and vibration, not to mention the view.

CONS Security and access to the tower could be a challenge.

887. While Wearing a Pair of Gravity Boots

You can really get creative with this. You can both wear gravity boots or just one of you for an interesting variation on 69.

BEST POSITION 69 or Bodyguard

PROS You can try some cool new standing positions.

CONS If you're upside down, all the blood will rush to your head.

888. In a Seven-Foot-Tall Champagne Glass Whirlpool Tub

Champagne is often used for celebration, so what better way to celebrate a night of passion than in a whirlpool tub champagne glass? Check it out at Caesar's Pocono Resorts in Pennsylvania: *www.caesarspoconoresorts.com.*

BEST POSITION Mastery or Doggy Style

PROS How cool is it to say you've had sex in a seven-foot-tall champagne glass?

CONS You can fall out of the glass, so be very careful not to get too rowdy!

889. By the Biggest Apple in Cornelia, GA

How can you resist an apple that is seven feet tall and twenty-two feet in circumference? Travel to this sightseeing spot and stop for some Adam and Eve action. Check it out at: *http://en.wikipedia.org/wiki/Cornelia,_Georgia*.

BEST POSITION Bodyguard or Standing Doggy Style

PROS You'll get to brag to your friends about doing it on top of the biggest apple ever. If you can't reach the top, no worries. Just take your picture naked beside the apple and put it in the photo album next to your naked picture with Big Tex.

CONS It's pretty touristy and probably not very private.

890. Inside the World's Smallest Church

There are little tiny churches all over America and the smallest one can be found in Oneida, New York. For this and other road trip ideas, check out Roadside America: *www.roadsideamerica.com/set/church.html*.

BEST POSITION Missionary or Spoons

PROS These little churches are just big enough for two.

CONS You may offend someone else's religious beliefs.

891. In a Submarine

Take a deep-sea voyage with your partner and see how wet you can get when you're hundreds of feet below the water's surface!

BEST POSITION Missionary or Cowgirl

PROS You can find a two-man submarine to charter for a few hours so that you're not disturbed.

CONS Submarines are fairly small, so you might have a little trouble maneuvering.

892. At Wayfarer's Chapel in Rancho Palos Verdes, CA

This chapel is absolutely gorgeous. If you don't get a sense of awe and wonder when you step inside, then just skip to the next place. Check it out at: *www.wayfarerschapel.org.*

BEST POSITION Missionary or Doggy Style

PROS The chapel brings together the beauty of modern architecture and the natural beauty of nature.

CONS You may have to get married there to get in!

893. In the Simpsons' House Replica in Henderson, NV

You'll have to get permission from the owner, but you never know until you ask.

BEST POSITION Missionary or Cowgirl

PROS It's a totally unique place to have sex.

CONS Doh!

894. A Sensory Deprivation Tank Filled with Saline

Imagine connecting with your lover in an entirely new way by having sex in total silence. The only sounds you'll hear are your breathing and the beating of your hearts.

BEST POSITION Standing Doggy Style or Dancer

PROS It's an incredible way to connect on a very deep and intimate level.

CONS It'll be totally dark.

895. In a NASA Zero-Gravity Chamber

The astronauts are testing sex positions in space—why can't you?

BEST POSITION Missionary or Cowgirl

PROS You'll last longer (at least physically) because your muscles will not fatigue so quickly.

CONS Many positions may not work because they depend on a certain amount of gravity.

896. At Area 51, Somewhere in Southern NV

Area 51 is the nickname for a military base located in the southern portion of Nevada. Because of the secret nature of the work done at the base, it's often the subject of conspiracy theories and UFO stories. If you can find it or get close to it, why not have some fun, extraterrestrial sex? You probably won't get close enough to Area 51 to lean up against any UFOs, but laying a blanket on the ground is enough to suffice.

BEST POSITION Anything goes at area 51!

PROS How cool is it to have sex in the most paranormal area in America?

CONS The government may catch you.

897. Chalk-Covered Street

The sidewalks of Chalk La Strada in La Jolla, California, are often beautiful and artistic. Celebrate these gorgeous works of art in your own way by making love on top! If you can't make it to California, cover your driveway with chalk drawings and then roll around naked. Check out the home of sidewalk chalk drawings at: *www.chalklastrada.com*.

BEST POSITION Missionary and Spoons

PROS You can indulge your artistic and creative side.

CONS If you make the trip to California, you'll be in a public place—so to get away with randy action, wait until closer to evening when fewer people are there.

898. Inside of a Parade Float

Have some private sex inside the float while spectators cheer along side. It'll be like they're cheering you on!

BEST POSITION Mastery and Missionary

PROS No one will even know you're there.

CONS You may be in a tight, cramped space for an extended amount of time. Once the parade starts, you're there until the end.

899. On the Ledge of a Billboard

Dress up like the guys who hang the billboards and no one will even give you a second glance. Just be careful getting up there and not falling off!

BEST POSITION Standing Doggy Style or Bodyguard

PROS This is a great example of just how much you can do in plain sight without anyone really seeing you!

CONS You may end up on the evening news. Keep an eye out for traffic helicopters.

900. On Top of a Giant Pumpkin

Did you know that there are contests every year to see who can grow the biggest pumpkin? In 2008, the winner pumpkin was more than 1,600 pounds! Why not take advantage of autumn's bounty with your lover? Find big pumpkins in your area at: *www.backyardgardener.com/pumkin .html.*

BEST POSITION Standing Doggy Style

PROS How many of your friends can claim that they had sex on a giant pumpkin?

CONS Make sure the pumpkin is not rotten or you'll sink in and ruin the shape of it! There'll be one irate farmer because these people take their pumpkins very seriously.

901. In a Gingerbread House

The Mall of America in Minnesota was home to the world's largest gingerbread house in 2007. Maybe they'll do it again? If not, search around during Christmas time and you're bound to find a giant gingerbread house somewhere. Or if you're really adventurous, build your own in the garage! You can even charge admission.

BEST POSITION Missionary or Doggy Style

PROS You'll be able to enjoy the sweet smell of gingerbread and frosting.

CONS It won't last forever so enjoy it while you can.

CHAPTER 24

100 CITIES
THAT
SCREAM SEX

Here's an extension on the Tour of America. While you're touring all fifty states, here are some cities and towns that you just can't miss! As you read through this list, see if you're left with a feeling of "What were they thinking?" and maybe even "When are we going?"

902. Assawoman, VA

Enjoy your woman's ass in Assawoman.

BEST POSITION Doggy Style or Rear Entry

903. Ball Bluff, MN

Give your man some oral in Ball Bluff.

BEST POSITION Standing Oral or Game's On

904. Ballstown, IN

Another great city in which to celebrate the male form.

BEST POSITION Standing Oral or Game's On

905. Bangs Beach, ME

Get banged at Bangs Beach.

BEST POSITION Deep Stick or Drill

906. Beaver Bay, MN

You can tour the country enjoying her beaver as you're about to see!

BEST POSITION Spread Eagle or Riding the Face

907. Beaver Crossing, NE

Enjoy her beaver some more in Beaver Crossing.

BEST POSITION Spread Eagle or Riding the Face

908. Beaver, AK

And again in Beaver, Arkansas.

BEST POSITION Spread Eagle or Riding the Face

909. Beaver, OK

And again in Beaver, Oklahoma.

BEST POSITION Spread Eagle or Riding the Face

910. Beaver, PA

And again in Beaver, Pennsylvania.

BEST POSITION Spread Eagle or Riding the Face

911. Beaver, UT

And again in Beaver, Utah.

BEST POSITION Spread Eagle or Riding the Face

912. Beaver, WV

And again in Beaver, West Virginia.
BEST POSITION Spread Eagle or Riding the Face

913. Beaverlick, KY

And again in Beaverlick, Kentucky.
BEST POSITION Spread Eagle or Riding the Face

914. Beaverville, NJ

And again in Beaverville, New Jersey.
BEST POSITION Spread Eagle or Riding the Face

915. Big Beaver Valley, WA

And again in Big Beaver Valley, Washington.
BEST POSITION Spread Eagle or Riding the Face

916. Big Bone Lick, OH

Finally, it's his turn! And we thought it was all about her . . .
BEST POSITION Game's On or Standing Oral

917. Big Lick, KY

His turn again!
BEST POSITION Game's On or Standing Oral

918. Big Lick, NC

His turn again!
BEST POSITION Game's On or Standing Oral

919. Big Lick, TN

His turn again!
BEST POSITION Game's On or Standing Oral

920. Big Lick, TN

His turn again!
BEST POSITION Game's On or Standing Oral

921. Blowtown, PA

Still his turn!
BEST POSITION Game's On or Standing Oral

922. Blue Ball, PA

You may want to skip Blue Ball or take matters into your own hands . . .
BEST POSITION Manual Stimulation

923. Cherry, MN

By now, it's too late for this one, but you can pretend!
BEST POSITION Missionary

924. Climax Springs, MO

Enjoy Climax over, and over, and over . . . all across the country!
BEST POSITION Try them all to find what works the best.

925. Climax, AL

Still enjoying climax . . .
BEST POSITION Your favorite position!

926. Climax, CO

Still enjoying climax . . .
BEST POSITION Your favorite position!

927. Climax, GA

Still enjoying climax . . .
BEST POSITION Your favorite position!

928. Climax, KS

Still enjoying climax . . .
BEST POSITION Your favorite position!

929. Climax, MI

Still enjoying climax . . .
BEST POSITION Your favorite position!

930. Climax, MN

Still enjoying climax . . .
BEST POSITION Your favorite position!

931. Climax, NC

Still enjoying climax . . .
BEST POSITION Your favorite position!

932. Climax, PA

Still enjoying climax . . .
BEST POSITION Your favorite position!

933. Climax, TX

Still enjoying climax . . .
BEST POSITION Your favorite position!

934. Cooter, MO

Okay, let's get started again! Back to her cooter . . .
BEST POSITION Spread Eagle or Riding the Face

935. Coxsackie, NY

His turn again!
BEST POSITION Game's On or Standing Oral

936. Cumming, GA

And all together . . . .
BEST POSITION Your favorite position!

937. Deep Gap, NC

Dive into the deep gap . . .
BEST POSITION Deep Stick or Spread Eagle

938. Deep Tunnel, NM

Take a ride in the tunnel of love.
BEST POSITION Doggy Style or Rear Entry

939. Desire, PA

Celebrate desire in Desire, Pennsylvania.
BEST POSITION Celebrate them all!

940. Dick, MI

Enjoy Dick, Michigan.
BEST POSITION Your favorite position!

941. Dickeyville, WI

Hoorah for Dickeyville—although it sounds like a pet name or something.
BEST POSITION Your favorite position!

942. Dicktown, NJ

It's time to visit Dicktown, New Jersey.

BEST POSITION Your favorite position

943. Dripping Springs, AR

Did your brain go where mine did? Shame on you!

BEST POSITION Spread Eagle or Riding the Face

944. Dry Beaver Creek, AZ

This is a city that you won't want to visit too often! Bring the lube . . .

BEST POSITION None without lube

945. Fingerville, SC

If you visit Fingerville, you may not need to visit Dry Beaver Creek at all.

BEST POSITION Manual Stimulation

946. Fort Dick, CA

Stand up and "salute"!

BEST POSITION Standing Oral

947. French Lick, IN

Another place to visit to avoid passing through Dry Beaver Creek.

BEST POSITION Spread Eagle or Ride the Face

948. Hooker Corner, IN

Hmmm . . .

BEST POSITION Whatever your partner agrees to . . .

949. Hooker Point, FL

Is there something missing here?

BEST POSITION Whatever your partner agrees to . . .

950. Hooker, OK

And again . . .

BEST POSITION Whatever your partner agrees to . . .

951. Hopeulikit, GA

Pronounce this one "Hope You Lick It."

BEST POSITION Game's On or Standing Oral

952. Hornytown, NC

Now you're talking. Visit Hornytown often!
BEST POSITION All of them

953. Hump Mountain, NC

North Carolina is sounding better and better!
BEST POSITION Missionary or Doggy Style

954. Humpy Creek, AK

Humpy, Humpy . . . Why does that make me think of rabbits?
BEST POSITION Missionary or Doggy Style

955. Intercourse, PA

How can you not have sex here?
BEST POSITION Missionary or Cowgirl

956. Ironwood, MI

The ladies love Ironwood!
BEST POSITION Any position as long as it lasts . . .

957. Johnson, FL

Enjoy your time with Johnson.
BEST POSITION Standing Oral or Game's On

958. Jugtown, NC

Celebrate your jugs in Jugtown.
BEST POSITION Cowgirl or Lotus

959. Kissimmee, FL

Kissimme all over and over again.
BEST POSITION Spread Eagle or Game's On

960. Latexo, TN

Is this where they make the condoms?
BEST POSITION Missionary or Cowgirl

961. Lay, CO

Have a good lay in Lay, Colorado!
BEST POSITION Missionary or Cowgirl

962. Leggtown, AL

Is she really all legs?
BEST POSITION Spread Eagle or Deep Stick

963. Licking, MO

She takes a licking and keeps on ticking.
BEST POSITION Spread Eagle

964. Longwood, FL

Ladies, rejoice!
BEST POSITION Deep Stick or Butterfly

965. Love Ladies, NJ

We all love the ladies, so let's "love" the ladies.
BEST POSITION Spread Eagle or Deep Stick

966. Love, AL

Fall in love in Love, AL.
BEST POSITION Missionary or Lotus

967. Loveland, IA

Fall in love again in Loveland, Iowa.
BEST POSITION Missionary or Lotus

968. Love, AZ

Fall in love again in Love, Arizona.
BEST POSITION Missionary or Lotus

969. Love, IL

Fall in Love again in Love, Illinois.
BEST POSITION Missionary or Lotus

970. Lovelady, TX

It's time to "love" your lady again.
BEST POSITION Missionary or Lotus

971. Loveland, OH

Everyone's in love in Loveland.
BEST POSITION Missionary or Lotus

972. Loves Park, IL

Make love in the park in Loves Park.

BEST POSITION Missionary or Cowgirl

973. Loving, KY

Make love in Loving.

BEST POSITION Missionary or Deck Chair

974. Mianus, CT

Really? What were they thinking?

BEST POSITION Rear Entry of course

975. Middlesex Beach, DE

Actually, awesome sex is better . . .

BEST POSITION Missionary or Deck Chair

976. Mount Joy, DE

I don't know, Joy, but I'm game if you are.

BEST POSITION Doggy Style or Standing Doggy Style

977. Needmore, FL

Still need more sex? Get it in Needmore.

BEST POSITION Deep Stick or Dancer

978. Nipple, UT

Time to celebrate those beautiful nipples . . .

BEST POSITION Standing Doggy Style or Lotus

979. Ogle, IL

Ogle her body in Ogle.

BEST POSITION Standing Doggy Style or Dancer

980. Olustee, FL

"Oh how I lust thee . . ."

BEST POSITION Cowgirl or Butterfly

981. Oral, SD

Time for some oral action in Oral.

BEST POSITION Spread Eagle or Game's On

982. Puseyville, PA

Did they really think we weren't going to add another *s*?
BEST POSITION Spread Eagle or Riding the Face

983. Scotrun, PA

And again . . . how could we not associate this one?
BEST POSITION Game's On or Oral Therapy

984. Seaman, OH

Release your semen in Seaman.
BEST POSITION Missionary or Manual Stimulation

985. Seman, AL

Didn't get enough the first time? Do it again.
BEST POSITION Missionary or Manual Stimulation

986. Sensation, AR

Feel some new sensations in Sensation.
BEST POSITION 69 or Rear Entry

987. Sexton, AR

Have a ton of sex in Sexton.
BEST POSITION Try them all.

988. Shafter, TX

Shaft her in Shafter.
BEST POSITION Rear Entry or Doggy Style

989. Slicklizzard, AL

Get your lizard slick in Slicklizzard.
BEST POSITION Game's On or Missionary

990. Spread Eagle, WI

Is there really more to say on this one?
BEST POSITION Spread Eagle of course

991. Sweet Lips, TN

Ah . . . her sweet, sweet lips . . .
BEST POSITION Spread Eagle or Riding the Face

992. The X, MA

Did they mean XXX?

BEST POSITION Try them all just in case.

993. Threeway, AZ

Sweet—a threeway in Threeway!

BEST POSITION Use a combination of positions for three.

994. Threeway, VA

Sweet—another threeway in Threeway!

BEST POSITION Use a combination of positions for three.

995. Unicorn, MD

We've finally found where the unicorns live. It's not a myth.

BEST POSITION Let her choose.

996. Unicorn, PA

Wait, don't all the unicorns live in Maryland?

BEST POSITION Let her choose.

997. Virgin, UT

You can pretend, can't you?

BEST POSITION Missionary

998. Virginville, PA

Is this where they hide them?

BEST POSITION Missionary

999. Vixen, LA

Now that's what I'm talking about.

BEST POSITION Try them all.

1000. Wacker, IL

This must be where all the single guys live.

BEST POSITION Manual Stimulation

1001. Wanker's Corner, OR

This is where the single guys go on vacation.

BEST POSITION Manual Stimulation

APPENDIX A

Our Top Twenty-Five Sex Positions

A big thank you to *www.sexinfo101.com*! All the positions and descriptions in this chapter, as well as many more, can be found on their site. They have the best illustrated and most comprehensive list of sex positions we've seen anywhere. When you visit the website, you can get a 3-D animated demonstration of the correct way to execute each of the positions below.

These are the twenty-five positions that we feel are mandatory reading for everyone. They are the basics, so it's worth taking the time to master each of these positions. What is not listed here is "Manual Stimulation." We figure that you're all very familiar with that particular position and will know exactly what we're talking about when we suggest it.

Positions are listed in alphabetical order.

69 The 69 sex position is considered one of the best oral intercourse positions, as it allows both partners to stimulate each other at the same time. Since the smaller partner may not enjoy having a substantially larger partner on top, we recommend the larger partner be on bottom.

ATTEN-HUT (STANDING ORAL FOR HIM) Incredibly versatile in terms of locations where it can be performed, frequent visits to the Atten-hut (Standing Fellatio) position are a part of every man's ideal life. The receiver simply stands or leans against a wall while their partner performs oral on them from a kneeling position. The position offers great access to the receiver's scrotum and anus (if they are okay with some anal play).

BODYGUARD The Bodyguard is a spooning position with all the intensity of Doggy Style, the connectivity of a side-by-side position, and the eroticism that comes with the uniqueness of all of the standing positions. To get into this position, the receiver simply stands in front and is penetrated from behind. This position is especially good in allowing the giving partner access to touch and caress the other's body, so make sure to keep those hands occupied!

BUTTERFLY The Butterfly position is at the head of the Butterfly family. It's great for the edge of the bed, couch, or just about any edge for that matter! To get into this position, the receiver lies back on just about any edge big enough and plants their feet on the floor, while the penetrating partner stands or kneels between their legs.

This position is very comfortable for both partners, though a pillow under the knees could be useful for a kneeling penetrator. In addition, added Manual Stimulation can be performed on the receiving partner by either partner without much difficulty, so make sure to try it out . . .

COWGIRL In the very popular Cowgirl position the receiver kneels astride the giver and leans forward on their arms; the giver is laid back. The receiver has much more control over depth and angle of penetration—a must-have for good G-spot stimulation. This position is definitely a must for your repertoire!

CRADLE In the Cradle position, the receiver's feet and arms are behind/below him or her to hold the upper body off the bed or couch, while the giver partner enters from a kneeling position.

The only difficult part of this sex position is aligning the genitals, which can be quite a problem for some couples. The easiest fixes are: standing on a stair, foot stool, couch cushion, or, if you are up to it, maybe some heels.

DANCER A unique twist on the Standing Missionary position, the Dancer is a lot of fun if you are looking for something with more face-to-face contact. Both partners simply stand facing each other, and the receiver raises one of their legs to give easier access while their partner helps support it. If the receiver is very flexible, you may want to try putting the raised leg onto the shoulder of the giver for an even more erotic experience.

DECK CHAIR To get into the Deck Chair position, the receiver lies on his or her back, pivots the hips so that the legs are in the air, and then bends the knees while the giver enters from a kneeling position while supporting some weight on the receiver's legs. A favorite of many men because of the sense of power that comes from folding their partner, the position definitely doesn't leave the receiver out. When the giver leans on the receiver's legs, it improves the angle of penetration to better target the G-spot or prostate gland. (For the more flexible, the receiver can pivot the hips higher to place the calves on the giver's shoulders).

DEEP IMPACT An easier variation of Deep Stick, as the giver kneels by the side of the bed or couch, thereby lining up more easily with the receiver. To get into the Deep Impact position, the receiver lies on her back with her legs resting on the partner's shoulders. The partner enters from a kneeling position. This position also holds true to its name, meaning the giver can penetrate deeply, unless of course he is too big. Any height difference (and discomfort for the giver) can be easily remedied using pillows.

DEEP STICK To get into the Deep Stick position, the receiver lies on her back with her legs resting on the shoulders of her partner, who enters from a kneeling position. Titled the Deep Stick, this position holds true to its name, meaning the giver can penetrate deeply, unless of course is too big. Although the position is versatile in terms of locations it can be performed, it can be very difficult for the giver if the genital altitude difference isn't corrected for, which thankfully can be done easily using pillows.

DELIGHT Similar to the Butterfly position, the Delight is an intimate position. The receiver sits at the very edge of a bed, couch, etc. while her partner kneels on the floor between her legs and enters. If you find that your alignment is off, use pillows under the receiver's bottom, or under the giver's knees, to adjust as needed.

DOGGY STYLE The most traditional version of the Doggy Style position is straightforward; the receiver on all fours with her partner holding on to the receiver's bottom or sides. Although Doggy Style is a huge hit with just about every guy, some women need time to open up to it due to the lack of face-to-face contact. That being said, once they do, they usually become big fans of it as well. There are many direct variations of Doggy Style, some of the more common are:

- Both partners standing
- Lowering the receiver's chest so that it is resting on the couch or bed
- The receiver's chest on the bed, but their knees on the floor

STANDING DOGGY STYLE In a venue where lying down is undesirable, this is a great position to practice. It is highly advised that the receiver find a suitably secure object to hold onto or balance herself against; this will allow for a more enjoyable experience, faster thrusting, and less likelihood of falling over. For variation, the receiver should try spreading her legs apart or bringing them together. However, the farther she spreads her legs, the deeper the giver is going to have to squat to gain access; say hello to burning quads. To overcome height differences, the giver should try squatting, or the receiver should be given something to stand on.

DRILL To get into the Drill position, the receiver lies on her back and wraps her legs around their partner who mounts from above. Although it is very similar to the Missionary position, the raised legs make a significant improvement in the penetration angle as well as the intimacy of the position, making it a good first step for improving the sometimes monotonous starting position.

GAME'S ON (ORAL FOR HIM OR HER) This version of fellatio is called Game's On; the receiving partner simply sits back while his or her partner performs oral from a kneeling position. Although not overly intimate with regard to other body parts, it is a great treat for the receiver.

Note: not everyone likes to have his or her head palmed (pulled forward) while they are performing, so if your partner doesn't like this it's in your best interest not to. If you have to do something, help keep their hair out of his or her mouth.

LAP DANCE The Lap Dance (previously known as Reverse Mastery) position is one of the highest rated; it puts the receiver on top while keeping penetration mobility high, and it's rear entry while remaining very intimate. To get into the position, the receiver sits, facing away, on top of the sitting partner.

The Lap Dance position is incredibly versatile, so make sure to experiment with it on other furniture. Here are a few ideas to help get those creative juices flowing: a bed, stairs, or the edge of the bathtub.

LEG GLIDER Since their research concluded without finding an existing name for this position, the folks at *www.sexinfo101.com* were privileged to name it the Leg Glider. Although it is considered extremely difficult by the inflexible, it is a massive hit amongst virtually all who can do it. The receiver simply lies on their side, with their upper leg pointed toward the sky or against the giver's shoulder, while their partner enters using a kneeling position.

LOTUS To get into the position, the giver sits cross-legged (Lotus-style) while the receiver sits into his lap facing him. The receiver wraps her legs around the giver; both wrap their arms around each other for support. This provides a good angle for penetration.

The giver and receiver together set up a rocking (fluid) motion to gain movement during penetration.

MASTERY With great face-to-face contact, Mastery is a very intimate position that's great for those who like to do a lot of kissing during intercourse. To get into the position the receiver simply sits on her sitting partner facing them. Unfortunately, the position isn't great for generating vertical movement, so if you want to experience the full effect, make sure to try it on a stool or chair that lets the receiver get a good footing.

MISSIONARY The Missionary position is probably the most common first position people try, which is probably related to its simplicity and the high level of intimacy experienced. To get into the position, the receiver simply lies down on her back while their partner lies face-down on top of her. Although aiming can be a little difficult at first for the giver, it doesn't take long to master this arrangement.

ORAL THERAPY (ORAL FOR HIM) If men had to choose one way to spend the rest of their lives, this would probably be it: Oral Therapy. It combines two of their greatest pleasures in life: receiving oral sex and lying down. The receiving partner simply lies back while their partner performs oral from a kneeling position. Although not overly intimate, it is a great treat for the receiver . . . Note: not everyone likes to have her head palmed while she is performing, so if your partner doesn't like this, it's in your best interest not to. If you have to do something, help keep her hair out of her mouth.

REAR ENTRY Essentially a rotated form of the Spoons position, the Rear Entry position is both hot and intimate. There are two main ways to engage in rear-entry sex. The receiver can either have her legs apart (as shown here) and with their partner's legs between them, or they can have their legs almost closed with their partner's legs on the outside. Although the first method provides easier access, and therefore deeper penetration, the latter positions the penis or strap-on at an angle for better stimulation of the G-spot or prostate gland.

The receiver's buttocks should be pushed up in the air, like a small hump. If entry is difficult, try placing a pillow under the receiver's pelvis. Also, while the giver is mounted on the receiver, the receiver can masturbate.

RIDING THE FACE (ORAL FOR HER) All the pleasure and control of Cowgirl also comes in the oral flavor via the Riding the Face sex position. The performing partner lies back on a bed or the floor and has their partner kneel over their face. The position is popular because the receiver has a great deal of control of what their partner is doing; they can lower their body for more pressure, raise it for less pressure, or rock forward and backward to change the area of focus.

SPOONS A great introduction to the world of rear-entry positions, it is very difficult to find someone who doesn't have Spoons in their favorite list. To get into the spooning position, the receiver lies on their side with their partner entering from behind. Not only is this position very intimate, but the penetration angle is great for either G-spot or prostate gland stimulation.

SPREAD EAGLE (ORAL FOR HER) In the Spread Eagle variation of cunnilingus, the receiving partner lies on her back with her feet planted to either side of the shoulders of the performing partner. This position is a big hit for its high level of comfort and the additional hand stimulation that can be provided. Because of the lack of contact from other parts of the body the experience can (ironically) be even more intense for the receiver, as all sensation can be focused on the highly sensitive groin area (if desired).

APPENDIX B

Ecstasy Quiz: How Comfortable Are You in Your Sexuality?

Take this short quiz to find out how comfortable you are in your sexual skin.

1. **I think of having sex as**
   a. Another demand I must meet
   b. A chore
   c. Something I have to get the "energy" for
   d. A pleasurable experience
   e. Great fun and I would never miss a chance to play!

2. **How do you feel about sleeping naked?**
   a. Eeewwww!
   b. I get too cold
   c. But he or she might want to have sex!
   d. Okay, but not every night
   e. Why would any one wear pajamas?

3. **Do you keep secrets from your partner?**
   a. Putting it all out there is dangerous
   b. A little mystery keeps it interesting
   c. I don't intend to but I "forget" to tell some things
   d. There is little my partner doesn't know about me
   e. My partner knows everything there is to know about me!

4. **Affection and sex**
   a. Hugging and kissing are not for me
   b. I always get aroused when being affectionate with someone
   c. Affection and sex are completely separate
   d. A little affection is okay but too much just feels icky
   e. Affection is an important part of my relationship, and doesn't always mean sex

5. **During lovemaking, I**
   a. Try to be as quiet as possible
   b. Struggle to allow my partner to know I am having a good time
   c. Tell my partner what I like beforehand
   d. Make small sounds to show I am enjoying myself
   e. Let it all out, with deep gut-level expressions of joy

6. **When my partner wants to have sex and I don't, I**
   a. Get pissed off; they should know I am not in the mood!
   b. Make up an excuse not to
   c. Go along with it and fake an orgasm
   d. Enjoy the touch and connection and let it put me in the mood sometimes
   e. Er, I never DON'T want it . . . I don't get the question

7. **During lovemaking, I**
   a. Keep the lights out
   b. Prefer to keep my eyes closed
   c. Use fantasies to keep it going
   d. Enjoy having dim light and seeing our bodies together
   e. Wow, turn on the lights and record this on video!

8. **When making love, I**
   a. Struggle to stay in the moment and focused on my partner
   b. Feel pressure to please my partner
   c. Am conscious of my own need for pleasure
   d. Experience occasional drifts of awareness from the moment
   e. Maintain pure focus, in "flow" with my partner's experience

9. **Have you ever been so excited you were willing to risk being caught?**
   a. Oh, no, it's not worth the possible embarrassment!
   b. I'd make love on the side of the road (in or behind my car)
   c. I'd do it in a public bathroom
   d. I'd have oral sex while I am driving
   e. I'd do it in a hallway, behind a building, anyplace I can find!

10. **Have you found yourself doing something sexually you couldn't believe you were doing?**
    a. No way, missionary is all I ever need
    b. I'll try anything natural once
    c. I'll try anything once
    d. Once in a while something new is nice
    e. Variety is the spice of life—the more the better!

SCORING

a = 1
b = 2
c = 3
d = 4
e = 5

0–10 POINTS: PLEASURE ANOREXIC Emotionally and physically blocked from experiencing pleasure. You need help discovering that you can not only tolerate, but also enjoy the thrill of pleasure.

Look for places with 🔥 🔥 or less.

10–20 POINTS: PLEASURE PHOBIC Too much pleasure scares you, you don't allow yourself to indulge in pleasure in most areas of your life, but certainly not in the intimate arena.

Look for places with 🔥 🔥 🔥 or less.

20–40 POINTS: PLEASURE TOLERATOR You are comfortable with a certain level of pleasure and ecstasy is something you dream of, though you don't see it as something possible for you.

Look for places with 🔥 🔥 🔥 🔥 or less.

40–50 POINTS: ECSTATIC LOVER You have little or no difficulty allowing yourself to indulge in pleasure to its fullest and you know how to let go and play with love and life.

Look for places with 🔥 🔥 🔥 🔥 🔥 or less.

Quiz provided by Melody Brooke, MA, LPC, LMFT, *www.ThisIsGreatSex.com.*

APPENDIX C

Kink Quiz:
What's Your Kink Level?

Take this short quiz to determine just how kinky you really are.

1. **Where is the last place you had sex in your home?**
   a. I don't remember
   b. In my bedroom on the bed, of course
   c. On the kitchen table
   d. On my parent's or child's bed (without them present)
   e. On my parent's or child's bed (with them present)

2. **Do you have a fetish?**
   a. Um, NO
   b. Does having an iPhone count?
   c. I like fishnets and heels
   d. I like leather
   e. I like whiskey enemas

3. **What's the most interesting sex toy you own?**
   a. I don't own any sex toys
   b. My iRabbit
   c. My butt plug
   d. My under-the-bed restraint system
   e. My leather hood and ball gag

4. **What do you think of your genitals?**
   a. Gross
   b. Useful
   c. Exciting
   d. I have so many pictures of it, I should make a scrapbook
   e. Makes a great pin-cushion!

5. **What most closely matches your masturbation habits?**
   a. Never
   b. Once in a while
   c. 2–3 times a week
   d. 2–3 times a day
   e. I'm masturbating right this minute

6. **How many orgasms have you had this week?**
   a. None
   b. One
   c. 3–5
   d. More than a dozen
   e. With or without a person stepping on my head?

7. **Which of the following would you consider messy sex?**
   a. Sex is messy, period
   b. Oral
   c. When a woman female ejaculates
   d. Sploshing (sex with pudding, paint, etc.)
   e. Statutory rape

8. **What do you think of anal sex?**
   a. EXIT ONLY, eew yucky
   b. I've tried it a couple times; it kind of freaks me out
   c. I love it!
   d. I want to peg my man! (put on a strap-on and do HIM)
   e. I love anal fisting

9. **What's your opinion on pornography?**
   a. It's WRONG
   b. I like softcore porn
   c. I like hardcore porn
   d. I like extreme BDSM porn
   e. I like fantasy snuff films

10. When was the last time you were naked outdoors?

  a. Never

  b. Skinny dipping at night two summers ago

  c. Making love on the beach with people picnicking the next sand dune over

  d. Spent a week at a swinger's nudist resort this summer

  e. Sigh, I keep getting arrested

SCORING

MOSTLY As *Repressed:* Thinks sex is distasteful, doesn't recognize any fetishes or fantasies, thinks genitals are ugly, doesn't masturbate, and could easily do without sex.
Look for places with ♪♪ or less.

MOSTLY Bs *Vanilla:* Cuddling, standard sex positions, passionate lovemaking, oral, watching porn, monogamy, mutual masturbation, basic sex toys.
Look for places with ♪♪♪ or less.

MOSTLY Cs *Kinky:* Anal, bondage using silk ties and scarves, teacher/secretary/cop fantasy role playing, exploring female bisexuality, watching hardcore porn, taking pics/filming, female ejaculation, threesomes, foursomes, sex in places other than the bedroom, advanced sex toys, exploring fetishes (foot, hair, latex, lingerie, etc.).
Look for places with ♪♪♪♪ or less.

MOSTLY Ds *Perverted:* Rape and incest fantasy role playing, orgies, bondage involving rope, face f***ing, water sports, exploring male bisexuality, public sex (with an audience), fisting, double penetration, pegging, crazy sex toys (big dongs, strap-ons), sex in your parent's bed (without them present).
Look for places with ♪♪♪♪♪ or less.

MOSTLY Es *F***ed Up:* There's nothing you won't try! Bestiality, edge play (bukkake, gangbangs, blood play, blade play, breath play, needle play, cock 'n ball torture, electrocution, humiliation and objectification, caging, necrophilia), ball gags, masks, CBT (cock 'n ball torture), sex in a church or cemetery, sex in your parent's bed (with them present).

Quiz provided by The Beautiful Kind, Kink Expert, *www.TheBeautifulKind.com.*

APPENDIX D

References

www.AskDanAndJennifer.com
www.1funcity.com
www.4toybox.com
www.51wharf.com
www.americasbestonline.com
www.beertown.org/events/gabf/
www.bonnaroo.com
www.burningman.com
www.caesarspoconoresorts.com
www.caseyjonesminigolf.com
www.casitasdegila.com
www.chenahotsprings.com
www.emeraldcityhobbies.com
www.fantasuite.com
www.foxdream.com
www.georgiaaquarium.org
www.illinoisamishcountry.com
www.iniquityclub.com
www.lazyrivercruises.com
www.letsgo-hawaii.com/beaches/punaluu.html
www.mallofamerica.com
www.massbayguides.com
www.nascar.com
www.nationaltownwatch.org
www.navalaviationmuseum.org
www.radiocity.com
www.roadsideamerica.com
www.sexhonesty.com
www.sexinfo101.com
www.shibaricon.com
www.slangcity.com
www.spymuseum.org
www.swingfestevents.com
www.thealmightyguru.com/Pointless/Cities.html
www.wayfarerschapel.org
www.whenwegetthere.com
www.wikipedia.org

About the Authors

Dan and Jennifer are the founders *www.AskDanAndJennifer.com*, which has been referred to as "The Best & Most Popular Dating, Love, and Sex Advice Column on the Internet Today . . . "

AskDanAndJennifer.com has become the premier website about relationships and sexuality on the Internet. Dan and Jennifer, in addition to providing value themselves via their articles and videos, have brought together key experts in the areas of dating, love, and sex, making it the go-to destination for all things love and sex.

AskDanAndJennifer.com has achieved a reader base of more than 400,000 readers per month with a strong following from many highly successful authors and website owners. In addition, Dan and Jennifer are featured content providers for YouTube, Revver, and Veoh. Their videos receive more than 4,000,000 views every month.

In a time when society is changing and globalizing so rapidly, their perspective is the refreshing, nonjudgmental, nonbiased approach to relationships and sex that you've been waiting for.

Dan and Jennifer confidently and honestly approach the most difficult of questions about sex and relationships and do it in a way that is informative, approachable, and entertaining. From "What Is the One Single Fastest Way to End a Relationship?" to "Rough Sex and BDSM—Are You Nuts?" and everything in between—it's all there and it's all fun. It's not all how to do this or that, but rather, how to foster a more healthy and satisfying relationship, both with and without sex.

You've done it in your bedroom, your bathroom, and your backyard
FUN SPOTS? SURE!
HOT SPOTS? NOT QUITE...

TIME TO GET BUSY!

Enter to win a trip for two to the **GRAND CANYON**

SEND IN A PHOTO OF THE WILDEST PLACE YOU'VE HAD SEX IN AMERICA

As well as a 25-50 word description of the place and the 411 on how you ended up doing it there

THE ENTRY WITH THE MOST CREATIVITY WINS!

REMEMBER OUR CRITERIA! The winner will be picked based upon the *1,001 Best Places to Have Sex in America* guidelines.

WE'RE TALKING: The Ecstasy Factor, Calorie Burn, Kink Level, and Risk Factor.